7-FIGURE COACH

HOW TO CREATE A MILLION-DOLLAR COACHING BUSINESS WITH ONE HIGH-TICKET PROGRAM

TARA MULLARKEY

7-FIGURE COACH

All scripture quotations (unless otherwise noted) are from The Holy Bible, New Century Version®. Copyright © 2005 by Thomas Nelson, Inc.

ISBN:
Paperback: 978-1-951503-57-4
Ebook: 978-1-951503-58-1

Authorsunite.com

For women everywhere who want it all

CONTENTS

PART II
GOING TO MARKET

PART III
SCALING YOUR OFFER

PART IV
7-FIGURE HEART

"The only limitations you will ever have are the ones you put on yourself."

~ Anonymous ~

FOREWORD

For too long, women have been sold a bill of goods—a lie about "having it all." The lie we've been told for decades is that we *can* have career and business success, but it comes at a steep cost. You must be willing to work your fingers to the bone building a business the traditional way. This inevitably begins with the assumption you probably won't even turn much of a profit in your first year.

Even worse, the only path to success following the old way is by sacrificing the very freedoms you're trying to achieve in the first place—spending time with your family and friends, not to mention sacrificing your own health to get there. You must work harder, put in more time, manage your time more effectively, and say goodbye to all the things in life that matter most to you.

Why would anyone in their right mind think this is the way to achieve success? Sometimes it is because we haven't allowed ourselves to be empowered by better ways. We might think we aren't worthy because the struggles and challenges of life have brought us down to a low point. We might be afraid we don't "have what it takes." We've been lied to for so long we've come to believe the lie. Here's my response:

This lie stops right here, right now.
It stops now because you're going to read this book.

The good news is that a growing number of women have rejected the antiquated models of building a business, along with the stress and burnout they cause. They have stopped believing the lie and have found a better way to build a business. They have found the success and freedom you crave for yourself.

The women who have turned the tables are women like Tara Mullarkey. Like me, Tara has come to understand that in the digital age of the twenty-first century, building an incredibly successful business isn't rocket science—far from it. What it does take is following a clear process that has been proven to get results beyond your wildest dreams. I should know because I've done it myself as well with my own business.

When you get clear on what unique program you can offer, communicate clearly about how you'll meet the needs of your audience, and follow the steps of what Tara has outlined in *7-Figure Coach*, you'll be on your way to achieving the success and freedom you thought could never be yours. Blessings to you as you begin your journey!

—**Shanda Sumpter**
Queen Visionary of HeartCore Business
August 2021

INTRODUCTION

The warning signs were all around me. After working for the top hedge fund in the world and a Fortune 50 company after that, I wasn't blind to the 2009 global financial crisis that caused the most severe recession since the Great Depression of the 1930s. I wasn't immune either.

While riding on the Metro North train to Manhattan from Connecticut, I got a phone call from my boss. My boss never called. I could hear the trepidation in his voice the moment I picked up the phone.

"Tara," he said, "you're on the list and I am too." I was shocked, and so was he.

He then added that his boss, a twenty-year veteran with the Fortune 50 company, and our HR manager were on the layoff list too. He told me to go home and rest, and we would talk in the morning.

As I hit "end" on the call, I couldn't help but smile. This was exactly what I had been secretly hoping for. Actually, this is what I had been praying for and speaking into existence.

But what was I going to do now?

I tried to let the jolt sink in. In one month, I would be jobless. After seven committed years and recently completing my MBA in finance, I would be laid off in the worst job economy my generation had ever seen.

As the train entered the dark tunnel approaching Manhattan, the fears began to envelop me. I had an expensive shoebox apartment in the city, I owned a condo in Connecticut, a car—a lifestyle dependent on my multi-six-figure income.

What was I going to do?

How was I going to pay my bills?

All the security was gone.

The truth was that I was miserable in the corporate banking environment. My creativity was not embraced, my values not considered, the clocking in and out, and there was a complete lack of meaning that haunted my soul as the years went on, but it was consistent. It was safe.

Until it wasn't.

The next morning, I walked into a very somber exit interview. My boss's boss and the HR manager were there. They told me my position was no longer available, and they had to let me go. They explained my severance package and asked if I had any questions.

I smiled.

They look confused.

I wished them well considering the situation they were in as well, with over twenty years with the company, and walked out feeling the freest I had since I was a child.

I don't know if I would have ever mustered the courage to leave the "stable" corporate job my immigrant parents had dreamed for me. But God had a different plan, and although this brought up all my fears around security, the only thing to do was to have faith.

What's interesting is that we're in another global financial crisis, but my business generated more revenue in 2020 than in any previous year. Why? Because it's all online. It's global. And its sole purpose is to help women like me build a profitable business from their expertise to not only provide lifestyle income but also the time freedom to enjoy it.

"Nearly 3 million U.S. women have dropped out of the labor force in the past year," says Megan Cerullo in her February 5, 2021 article on CBSnews.com. And "women's labor force participation rate hit a 33-year low in January 2021," says Courtney Connley, in her February 8, 2021, article on CNBC.com.

This means millions of women are looking for an alternative way to generate income that allows them the flexibility to care for their families. But here's what I've noticed about expert women: They undervalue themselves, undercharge for their services, and overwork to the point of burnout without the financial results to show for it.

WHAT'S HOLDING YOU BACK?

There's an epidemic I've been studying for a while: Genius women hiding because they are living in fear.

They are afraid they will lose themselves, hustle too hard, not have enough time for their husband and kids, or become a slave to their business and their clients.

They're afraid to raise their prices for fear of what people will think of them.

They feel overwhelmed with posting on Instagram, YouTube, and Facebook day in and day out. They're working hard, but they're not gaining traction. They're getting burned out because they're not getting the results they want—or deserve.

Some may already be selling for higher prices, but they don't know where their next client is coming from. They do not have a system set up to get a client "on demand." They are posting and praying.

They are starting slow and low and thinking someday they'll craft the higher-end offer once they gain more experience.

In essence, they don't have a proven plan.

It's a shame because it's causing amazing women to miss out on living God's promise of purpose and prosperity in their lives.

I know this because I've lived it. And I've helped thousands of women work through it. I've been through the peaks and the valleys, the feast moments and the famine moments. I've led international retreats and big-ticket programs and have experienced all the highs and lows and everything in between.

Once I figured out how to implement what I'm sharing in this book, though, everything began to fall into place. I stopped suffering through the ups and downs. I stopped working every moment of every day. I started taking care of myself, getting enough rest, traveling for fun, dancing on the beach—I built my business around my desired lifestyle.

Financial freedom and time freedom don't come from working for someone else. Starting and growing an expert business that can be facilitated online is the best path to freedom.

Overcoming Fear

I've met with countless high-achieving women day in and day out for years. These are highly educated women who are successful by most standards, but they're holding themselves back.

For example, Beth has her master's degree and is a registered dietician and health coach. She decided to go all in on her online business in 2020.

After realizing that one-on-one sessions were never going to create the kind of lifestyle and financial freedom she craved for herself and her family, she decided to create an online course.

She priced the course at first for $297 then lowered it to $197 because she felt like it was too expensive. After months of preparation to make her course powerful, ten days to promote and "launch," countless hours of lost sleep, and missed time with her toddler, she didn't hit her goal of selling twenty women on this course.

She only got three women to sign up.

She barely made $1,000 and she felt exhausted.

She felt like a failure and started doubting whether she could even do this and whether this whole coaching business idea was going to work.

That's when she joined High Ticket Empress (HTE). Within a few weeks, she was able to package her expertise into just ONE signature program, raise her prices by a factor of ten, and book her first high-ticket clients.

She uses a simple three-step marketing system to bring her inbound high-ticket client leads while she sleeps.

Today she spends less time on her business, makes more money, and gets her clients better results than when she was offering one-on-one sessions. Not only is she able to invest back into her business but she is also able to pay herself well from it—for the first time in two years.

Packaging her expertise into one signature high-ticket program was an absolute game changer for her.

WHO IS THIS BOOK FOR?

If you are a personal trainer making $50K a year, you can make $1 million a year by developing a health coaching program, or you can develop a program teaching other health professionals how to build a local personal training business.

If you make $200K a year as a psychologist, you could develop an online program that triples or quadruples your income and allows you to take your work online and reach people nationwide and even globally.

If you have a lash or hair business and make $75K a year right now, you could develop an online group coaching program making a million or more teaching other stylists how to build out a full roster of clients.

If you are an attorney or a mediator specializing in immigration or divorce, you could create a premium online program teaching your process to get the results quicker or with less pain.

If you are an LCSW or a therapist making $100K trading eight hours a day for $150 an hour, you can make $1 million or more by developing an online program teaching other therapists how to structure their business, or you can create an online program for a specific niche of clients you help.

The key point in all these scenarios is that not only can you make more money, but you can also leverage your time. You can remove one-on-one face time with clients and instead facilitate one Zoom call a week and facilitate "one to many." You've just shaved hours off your workload and increased your income at the same time.

We're still in the early adopter time for online education even though it's not new. In fact, according to Global Market Insights (gminsights.com) in May 2021, e-learning "surpassed USD 250 billion" and is projected to reach $1 trillion in 2027. Online education has been growing exponentially over the past ten to fifteen years.

Right now, there is a two- to five-year window of incredible opportunity for experts.

Why? Because 2020 proved that online education is the future. It became widely accepted and adopted to learn online.

Children began to learn online via Zoom. Corporate structures and teams became remote, and they all communicated, were trained, and worked online. Even court cases and legal proceedings were held online using Zoom.

So, online education is the new way of learning in all spheres and industries. That means if you have an expertise, you have an incredible opportunity right now!

You must share your knowledge online. And if you are already online, you need to set yourself up to scale.

Why?

Because the market is going to become more saturated over the next two to five years. Your opportunity to dominate market share in your niche and industry is NOW.

There are people capitalizing on the online education model who are making multi-millions per year and millions per month. If you're still struggling, it's because you don't have the proper strategy. This book will teach you how to bring your expertise online and set you up to scale.

This book is about how 1 percent of online experts and coaches make it, while the others struggle. It will show clearly why and how the small percentage excel, the overwhelming majority fail, and some never even try.

FORMAL EDUCATION IS NOT THE PATH TO FINANCIAL FREEDOM

Formal education has failed us. People pay outrageous fees (and accrue high-interest loans) to attend prestigious colleges while learning from people who are not innovators or real creators in the real world. These professors earn $40K a year. How are they going to teach you how to become financially free?

Most graduates of colleges leave with a mountain of debt and no solid job pathway. What does a degree in English or Sociology get you?

Society has programmed us to think this is the path. In fact, our parents may have only dreamed we would go to college.

I started out on the traditional path. I'm the first person in my generation to get a graduate degree. My parents didn't finish high school, and my grandparents were cattle farmers in Ireland.

But the internet has changed everything for us. We can create courses to share our knowledge, or coach others on how to achieve something we have achieved.

Our information is now readily available to the world through the internet. The old methods no longer serve us, but we tend to fear the unknown—just like when the internet launched and people were skeptical, but now we can't imagine life without it.

The opportunity to sell your knowledge online is ripe right now. We are in goldmine times for online education.

SOCIAL POSTING IS NOT A BUSINESS MODEL

There's a belief that building an online education, coaching, or consulting business means you post on social media all day every day and the clients will come.

It's kind of like gathering for dinner or vino with girlfriends, only we're all on this path of living our purpose and making an online business out of it, so we're hanging out online. It's freakin' cool. What an amazing time we live in!

However, you see what's happening, right?

It's become a business "strategy" to post on Instagram, on YouTube, or in Facebook groups three to five times per day to get visible and get more clients. Does it work? It can, yes. Does it stress you out and make you a slave to your business? Emphatically, YES.

I talk to women every day whose only business strategy to get more clients is to become more visible. The thing they don't grasp is if you aren't converting the people who already see your posts, you aren't getting new clients.

So, their main strategy to accomplish visibility is to put themselves out there on social media. But most of them loathe the thought of this, so they procrastinate and become inconsistent.

Is this you? It used to be me! Let me tell you why this strategy sucks. If you hate it, you won't do it, and therefore you'll feel terrible about your business because you're not doing what you think you "should" be doing.

Even if you love it, and stay consistent, you are still doing manual labor to get clients, which keeps you a slave to your business forever. It's totally unrealistic to think you can come up with content three to five times per day for Instagram stories, reels, YouTube, and Facebook groups!

And never mind how emotionally draining and discouraging it is when you don't get any likes, comments, or reactions to your posts. You feel like you totally wasted time. And the truth is you did.

Let me tell you the good news: There is a better way! One that changes the game completely from chasing clients to having them come to you.

There are really only a few shifts you need to make to implement this automated system that brings you five, ten, or even twenty new high-ticket clients every month, and you don't even need to spend a lot on advertising.

This book will give you the key you're missing to take your expert business to consistent five-figure months and beyond.

WHO IS TARA MULLARKEY?

Before becoming an online business coach and the founder of High Ticket Empress, I worked on Wall Street in the corporate finance sector, where I underwrote, sold, and managed over $500 million in highly leveraged loans and worked for the largest hedge fund in the world, as well as a Fortune 50 company.

After graduating with an MBA and retiring from Wall Street and corporate America, I traveled much of the world including India, Thailand, Bali, Laos, Vietnam, Singapore, The Netherlands, England, Spain, France, Greece, Italy, Australia, New Zealand, Morocco, Hawaii, and Mexico. I settled for a while in Tulum, Mexico, where I began creating my online coaching business. Since then, I have been featured in *Forbes*, Huffington Post, *Yahoo Finance*, ABC, NBC, and Fox.

I launched my online coaching business in November 2012, but I was trying to figure it out on my own, so it wasn't until December 2014 that I had my first six-figure year working for myself. I now consistently hit six-figure *months* with a small team who are devoted to helping female experts create million-dollar businesses through one high-ticket online program without doing low-ticket course launches or one-on-one sessions.

Back in March 2015, I attended a high-level mastermind event for six- and seven-figure earners where I discovered that most of the coaches I met were actually broke, unhealthy, overworked, and not happy. That scared me into searching for ways to make my coaching business sustainable.

Within three months, I up-leveled my business strategy to include automated funnels and group masterminds. This way, I was able to leverage automation without sacrificing intimacy with my clients. That's when I started seeing a steady stream of clients coming in, month after month and year after year.

I've now sold multiple millions in coaching program sales over the past nine years and have worked with a range of six-, seven-, and eight-figure clients in more than twenty countries, including some of the top experts in their field.

Even though I'm experiencing financial freedom now, things weren't always this way. I grew up as a first-generation American. My parents had immigrated from Ireland to London when they were fifteen years old to find work. A year before I was born, they immigrated from London to the United States to make a better life.

I grew up in Connecticut with a lot of pressure to become successful. My parents were working-class and worked to pay the bills so we never went without, but they never really had much left over. When I was twelve years old, my parents divorced and my mom supported us on her own.

I learned to work from an early age and started working as soon as I legally could at fourteen years old. I worked through high school, bought my first car (a used VW red Jetta), and I worked while going to college. I ended up graduating with a degree in Economics, not because I loved the topic, but because I knew I could get a well-paying finance job with that degree.

I landed that well-paying job working for a company at the top of the Fortune 50 list. I worked as an analyst for corporate banking and we had a lot of fun—boondoggles in Vegas and Puerto Rico, stays at the Ritz Carlton in Naples, playing golf with our traders at the famous Baltusrol Golf Club in New Jersey and Monarch Beach Golf Links in Dana Point, California, and fancy dinners at Morton's. But deep down, I knew it lacked meaning for me.

My paycheck and bonuses kept growing, but my desire to do something meaningful was growing along with it. I attended a high-end master's program and got my MBA in finance. At the same time, my heart really wanted out. But I had built a lifestyle around my multiple six-figure income, so it was hard to think of walking away.

On my four-hour-a-day commute to and from work, I would find myself staring out the window of the train, knowing there had to be something more than this for me. I would think: *God has a plan for me, and this isn't it.*

As far back as I could remember, I had been fascinated when I heard people tell the real stories of their lives and how they were able to transform their painful situations into new opportunities for themselves. As early as eight years old, I remember going to church services and imagining myself as the preacher, helping people with their lives.

But how could I follow my heart AND make a living? How could I share my message AND fulfill my need for financial security? How could I make an impact on people AND live a big life?

That's when God intervened. I got laid off during the financial crisis of 2009, along with thousands of others.

This turned out to be a new beginning for me. I flew to Thailand with the intention to travel and see the world for five months. I ended up traveling around the world for three years—just me and my backpack.

I began my coaching business from a little casita I was renting by the beach in Tulum, Mexico. I started to study the online coaching and marketing space and created my first website way back in 2011.

I built the website and thought the clients would just come. Boy was I wrong.

I was the definition of "hustle."

- I was charging a mere $125/hour for my work.
- I was over-giving like a crazy woman because I was afraid of not being good enough.
- I charged only $197 for my first online course and got only four women to sign up. Sigh.
- I was sacrificing love and relationships to work on my business and make it grow.
- I was spending a lot of time doing "free work" because I wanted to serve the people who couldn't "afford" coaching.
- I was doing ALL. THE. THINGS. in my business from website updates to graphic design to doing sales calls to scheduling clients to writing posts to book-keeping, and the list goes on.

My biggest problem was that I was underselling myself, leaving MILLIONS on the table.

I would often think, *this is not sustainable. And what if I had kids right now? I wouldn't be the kind of mom I want to be.*

So, I became committed to find a way for me and for all women to hold their desire to be a wife and present mother, while also building a business and creating financial freedom for her family.

That's why I don't offer one-on-one sessions, make low-ticket offers, or teach women to do the same. I teach my students how to create one high-ticket signature program that brings transformational results.

I like to think of my business as my unique fingerprint. It's rare, and it only belongs to me. My business is my outward expression of who I am. It's the vessel I am using to share my gifts and impress upon this world the God-given texture of what my soul believes and how it wants to serve.

And for this, I am so thankful. I don't take any of it for granted. This is all a gift, and I plan on continuing to serve as many women as possible so they can give more, be more, and love themselves more.

How to Use This Book

This book is about how female coaches and consultants can create, grow, and scale a million-dollar expert business with just *one* high-ticket online program without sacrificing their family, health, or sanity.

Step 1: Create the offer

Step 2: Sell the program (proof of concept)

Step 3: Scale the program

I strongly recommend you read this book from cover to cover. Then, go back and read it again (or listen to it), implementing each of the tactics and strategies as you go.

This book will walk you through, step-by-step, how to focus on the fastest pathway to creating 7 figures with your expertise. It will help you avoid burnout, exhaustion, and self-sabotage. And it will show you why planning to become Instagram-famous or hoping for YouTube or Facebook group stardom is not a business plan.

I've broken the material into parts as each part builds upon the previous one:

- Part I: The Model
- Part II: Going to Market
- Part III: Scaling Your Offer
- Part IV: 7-Figure Heart

The first part, "The Model," is all about choosing your niche and creating one clear signature high-ticket offer.

The second part, "Going to Market" will show you how to charge and sell a high-ticket offer.

The third part, "Scaling Your Offer" is going to teach you how to set up inbound client lead generation and grow your income month after month, practically on autopilot.

Please don't feel like you got everything in the first three parts and skip the last part. The final "7-Figure Heart" part isn't last because it's the least important—just the opposite. It's the foundation for all the other parts and deserves your undivided attention. This part is critical to your success as a woman and is likely the reason you don't have the success you want yet.

When you get to the end of the book, be sure to download the digital assets in the Appendix: Bonus Resources. Watch the videos listed there. Take notes. If you need help, you can find other women on the same journey in our free 7-Figure Femme Facebook group: https://www.facebook.com/groups/7figurefemme/

Welcome to the family!

PART I

THE MODEL

1

HOW TO MAKE A MILLION FROM JUST ONE OFFER

If you set your goals ridiculously high and it's a failure, you will fail above everyone else's success.

—*James Cameron*

The sun was peeking through my office window early when I met Lisa on Zoom for a video conference. As soon as I opened the room on my screen, I could see the eagerness in her eyes.

I adjusted the ring light facing my Mac in my office so she could see me clearly. I knew she was a high achiever, highly educated, successful by most standards, yet flailing in her online coaching business.

She looked at me through our computer screens and teared up, "I wouldn't say I feel hopeless, but I'm barely surviving here."

I've met with countless Lisas over the years. They come to me exhausted, feeling like failures, and doubting whether they can do this, wondering whether this whole coaching business idea is going to work.

Within weeks, my team and I show them how to develop a method from their expertise and craft just ONE signature program, raise their prices by a factor of ten, and start booking high-ticket clients consistently.

BECOMING AN INSTAGRAM UNICORN IS NOT A SOLID STRATEGY

You and I both know the women who have 300,000 followers on Instagram and sell business courses teaching you how to create your own online empire.

Problem is, they are Unicorns.

Here's what I mean: Most people don't have 10,000 followers, never mind 450,000 followers.

And I'm not talking fake followers. They seem to have built a very engaged audience of hundreds of thousands.

Kudos to them. I'm not kidding. That is incredible!

Let's do the math for a second. When they launch a low-ticket course for $997 or $1,997, even if they sell to only 3% of their audience (which is industry standard), they will make millions on one launch!

300,000 x 3% = 9,000 people buying at $997 = ~$9-million-dollar launch

Incredible for them. But unrepeatable for you.

There is a better and faster way to make you profitable without waiting for the follower count on Instagram.

What Entrepreneurial Women Don't Know Is Killing Them

Plagued with the overwork and over-perform addiction, the entrepreneurial ambitious woman tends to meet everyone else's needs but her own.

Transfer this to her business and she's creating programs for all her different areas of expertise and hustling day and night on social media. Pretty soon she has a dozen low-ticket courses on her website that no one is buying.

Or worse, she might be "launching" a new course every month, spending hours upon hours marketing it on Instagram, YouTube, and Facebook by the start date, only to fall short of her goals once again, not getting enough new enrollments to even break even on her costs.

Do you know how many female entrepreneurs and coaches are out there creating new courses—NEW courses—every single month to meet their goals?

They want to keep their numbers going, and the only way they know how to do it is to keep creating a new course and hoping their current audience will buy into that new course the next month as well.

Never mind the overwhelm and exhaustion from the sales and marketing of a course launch, then she must deliver the course. This is particularly upsetting if she wanted fifty women to enroll and only got five to sign up. She now must fulfill on a course with negative profit margins.

Adding to the overwhelm is the fact the whole process must start again next month for her next course so she can try to meet her income goals.

What woman in her right mind would sign up for this madness?

She's not even making enough to pay a team to help her. Plus, she has kids running around at her feet, all while she is trying to post her next IG story, which likely won't even result in a $197 sale.

This woman doesn't understand how she's sitting on a gold mine. That her $197 course could really be a $5,000 transformational program.

HOW MANY HIGH-TICKET SALES DOES IT TAKE TO GET TO 7 FIGURES?

Let's talk numbers for a second.

It's important to understand why one signature high-end program—and structuring your business that way out of the gate from here on out—is the best thing to do.

If you want to reach 7 figures in a year, you need to sell approximately $83K per month. Let's say, for the sake of example, you want to generate half a million next year, which is $500K. This means you'll need to make, on average, $40K per month.

Even if you max yourself out doing eight one-on-one sessions per day at $150 an hour, five days a week, you'd make about $24,000 per month—and have no life.

Now, let's assume you're thinking you'll create an online course and sell it for $497.

How many course buyers do you think you need every single month to make $40K a month?

The answer is eighty (80). You need to sell eighty new people into your course every single month to achieve $40K months or half a million dollars per year.

Now, if that number doesn't scare you, let me break down how hard that is. You need to have a huge audience to get eighty people converted to buy on a sales page without ever talking to them, month after month.

It's a model requiring a lot of volume in order to make the profit you want.

Studies show that only three percent of people who see your sales page will convert. That means you need to have 2,700 people seeing your funnel or your sales page for that product *every single month.*

Even if you have 10,000 followers on IG, how many people see just one post? Usually just hundreds.

So that means you'll need to pay for those 2,700 people to see it, and that means paid advertising.

Increasing your advertising costs means your profit margins are going to be cut really small because of how much you need to spend to get eyes on your $497 product.

Now, let's say after you spend all that on advertising, you do the numbers, you break it down, and you spent $300 getting one sale. So that's $300 out of your $497.

That means you make $197 profit on every single person that comes in—and that's not taking out taxes. And then you must rinse and repeat and do another course launch the next month.

Now, let's contrast the eighty new students per month at $497 each with a high-ticket offer.

Let's say that you price your course at $5K and you structure your expertise as a high-end transformational program.

How many new clients per month do you need to reach your $40K-per-month goal? You need *eight*. Only eight new clients per month, which is two new clients per week. Do you think you could book two new clients per week? Even if you run paid advertising, your profit margin will still be high because you're offering a premium product.

These numbers work. It is so much more doable, and once you set up a system that's bringing you these leads, you can do it month in and month out.

This means your $40K month can become an $83K month ($1 million dollar run rate) by doubling your enrollments. Just sixteen (16) new clients a month at $5K gets you to 7 figures.

THE TOP SECRET OF THE 1-PERCENT EARNERS OF THE COACHING INDUSTRY WHO EARN $100,000 OR MORE PER MONTH

I had already been coaching for about two years when I decided to go to a big event in Las Vegas.

I was trying to figure out how to make my business work without overwhelming myself, working all the time, and never knowing where my next client was going to come from.

Did you know that 67 percent of coaches earn less than $2K per month? And that 88 percent earn less than $10K per month? The vast majority of coaches earn less than six figures a year!

Now, you might be thinking you would be very happy with $10K per month if you are still trying to get there.

But here is the interesting thing: 1 percent of coaches generate $100K or more per MONTH. These coaches and consultants have created high-profit, high-impact companies.

The $100+ billion coaching, transformational, and e-knowledge industry is going to *1 percent* of coaches. What do these 1-percenters have in common?

- Group coaching facilitation with one high-ticket signature program
- Automated client lead generation

They all had a high-end program and an automated system to bring them leads for their high-end program. That was it!

2

WHY "HIGH-TICKET" IS THE RIGHT TICKET

It's great to have a private jet. Anyone that tells you that having your own private jet isn't great is lying to you.

—*Oprah Winfrey*

Over New Year's this past year, I purchased a Yves Saint Laurent bag while visiting Las Vegas. This was not an impulse purchase; I had been thinking about this bag for a while. I started seeing other women carrying these bags with the beautiful gold YSL lettering, and I could feel myself inching toward this purchase.

Even though I had thought about this moment, I still felt nervous walking into the store. *Am I really going to spend this much on a bag? This bag is priced at over $2,000!*

Nowadays I'm grateful to say I have many Louis Vuitton, Yves San Laurent, Gucci, and Chanel bags, Christian Louboutin shoes, and other high-end accessories. I take care of these bags and shoes because they are luxury items. They are not easily replaceable. They even increase in value IF I take care of them. They can be resold for a price higher than what I paid.

Compare that to the throwaway bag from TJ Maxx. Nothing wrong with that purchase by the way, but let's face it, you won't care for a $50 bag like you will a $5,000 purchase.

People Value What They Pay Premium Prices For

When you invite your clients to buy your high-ticket offer, you're offering them a high-end transformation. If they invest in themselves at that level, they're going to take their transformation very seriously.

They're not going to buy your course and leave it on their digital shelf. They're not going to forget about it. They're going to dive in, do the work, and get the result.

What they're buying when they pay $5K-$25K or more to work with you is their end result.

Yes, they're buying your program. But really, they are buying accountability, your support, and your expertise, so they can achieve it faster following a proven path.

Online courses have become like the books you find at discount stores. The material isn't original. It's not transformational. They're not getting people the results they want. And in my experience, people are starting to become wary of buying yet another course they'll never finish.

How many courses do you have sitting on your hard drive right now?

And how many do you have log-in details to but haven't watched even one-third of the content?

Studies show that consumers are becoming weary of buying another online course only to let it sit on their hard drive. Consumers don't want more videos to watch, they want REAL transformation.

For those of you providing sessions: When clients pay for sessions with you, they're paying for *your time* instead of paying for *their transformation.*

With DIY courses that are lower-ticket items or pay-per-session clients, you're more likely to get clients who complain, ask for refunds, don't take their work seriously, and come back week after week not doing the work you asked them to do.

High-ticket clients, on the other hand, take responsibility for their actions. They almost never ask for refunds, and they take the homework seriously because they've made a significant investment from which they expect to get transformational results.

THE DIFFERENCE BETWEEN LOW-TICKET AND HIGH-TICKET OFFERS IN THE MARKETPLACE

Low-ticket courses sell additions or nice-to-haves. But high-ticket programs sell major transformations; they change people's lives.

Picture this: You've been struggling with back pain for years. You wake up in agonizing pain every morning. It is keeping you from doing the things you love. You look online and find a $197 course that will teach you how to cure all back pain.

Do you buy it? Hopefully not. Why? Because the promised result is not believable for the investment.

Does the course creator know your unique problem? Have they talked to you? Do they know when and how you got injured? Do you believe they can truly help you?

What are the chances they have a one-size-fits-all, do-it-yourself solution for a major problem like that?

Now, on the other hand, let's say you want to learn how to create Instagram reels. You know it would grow your following, and it's all the rage right now on Instagram. You come across a course for $47 that will teach you how to master reel creation. Do you buy it?

I sure hope so!

Instagram reels work the same for everyone. It is something that *can* be taught in a one-size-fits-all format for the masses. Reels will not radically change your life. Learning how to create them won't relieve a major pain like a possible divorce, a food addiction, a desire to change careers, or triple your sales, and that's why it will be successful as a low-ticket DIY course.

A high-ticket program that will succeed is the intersection of your expertise, a big problem the market wants to solve, and what you're passionate about.

THE HIGH-TICKET TEST

Maybe you're beginning to see the potential to have financial freedom *and* put your skills and knowledge to work helping others.

Usually, the problem is you can't zero in on a marketing niche that is just right for you. You know clarity is king in the online space, and what works to get referral clients does not work when you want to sell to a "cold" audience online.

If you've been doing this a while, you might have picked a niche, but you're still not seeing the response you want. This is because your messaging is off; it's likely not hitting the main pain point of your ideal client.

The magic in zeroing in on your high-ticket niche is two-fold: You have to be specific in who you help, and you must be very intimate with the tangible pain they are experiencing *right now*.

How do you know if your offer will withstand the high-ticket test? Your offer needs to meet the following three criteria:

1. It must promise a quantifiable end result. Clarity is the name of the game here. If your program's end result is not tangible, quantifiable, and clear, you are going to hear crickets.

2. Is it something people are buying right now? Is there a market for it? If nobody else is selling this right now, it may mean there is no market for it.

3. Is it life-transformational? Your program can't be an addition to someone's life, or a small addition, it actually has to solve a major problem for them. Think: Save time, make money, change careers, get healthy.

If your offer fulfills all three, then it passes the high-ticket test!

Pro tip: Most anything can be made into a high-ticket offer, it just may require you to expand your vision and belief in yourself!

WHY SOMEONE HIRES A
High Ticket Coach

- INABILITY TO DO IT ON THEIR OWN
- WANTS TO DO IT FASTER
- WANTS A PROVEN SYSTEM

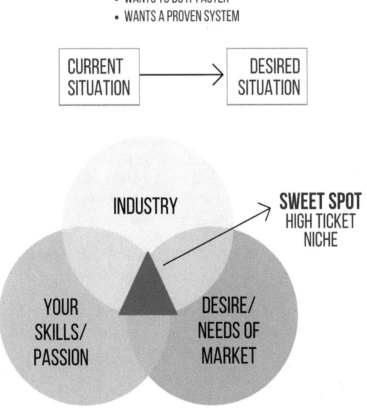

3

WHY PEOPLE LOVE YOU BUT DON'T BUY FROM YOU

Followers don't equal sales and 'likes' don't equal success.

—Unknown

When Emily applied to work with us in High Ticket Empress, she had about 20,000 engaged followers on Instagram and her revenue was barely $2,000 per month from long-time one-on-one clients.

Everyone LOVED Emily. 20,000 followers on IG is a big deal and quite a success!

Her posts were captivating. She'd get dozens and dozens of comments on each post.

But when she'd make an offer for her audience to buy or apply, she'd hear crickets.

No one bought her course.

No one booked a discovery call.

And when one discovery call would trickle in, they'd always say those dreaded words at the end, *"Emily, I just love you. Let me think about it and get back to you."*

Maybe you're beginning to see the potential to have financial freedom *and* put your skills and knowledge to work helping others. But how do you figure out that one high-ticket offer that people want?

Usually, the problem is that you can't zero in on a marketing niche and offer your clients will sign up for in droves. You have talents and a ton of certifications. You've lived lifetimes of experiences. And when it comes to getting your work out there, you make a huge mistake—*you try to help everybody, and thereby help nobody.*

It's not that you're lacking talent. It's not that you're not qualified. It's not that you can't create real transformation for people.

It's because your audience does not see the value in what you do and how it can solve a major problem for them right now.

You're the world's best kept secret.

If you don't articulate the power of what you do in a specific way, also known as finding your lane or choosing your niche, and communicate it powerfully, also known as messaging and marketing, then you likely will hear crickets when you make offers.

Here's how you clarify your unique niche in the marketplace so people buy:

1. You must be specific in the problem you solve in one of the three core human concerns.

2. You must be specific in *who* you help.

3. You must be very intimate with the pain they are experiencing *right now* that is motivating them to take action.

If you don't have this in place, then your business will suffer. Believe me, I tried it for years.

Followers don't equal sales.

THREE CORE HUMAN CONCERNS

There are three big online niches that really rock it in the coaching industry: money, love, and wellness.

These are the areas of life that keep people up at night.

When you think about it, every time you've invested big you wanted to SEE big results in your bank account, your body, or your relationship happiness.

It's just how we're wired.

Yes, your coaching and your program will guide them through the intangibles like the spiritual, energetic, emotional work you know is required to get your clients lasting change.

But the reality is this: People buy a quantifiable, tangible end result.

Money/career is tangible.

Relationship status is tangible.

Health is tangible.

Solutions That Sell

RELATIONSHIP	HEALTH	WEALTH
FINDING LOVE	HEALING DISEASE	MAKING MONEY
SAVING MARRIAGE	LOOKING BETTER	SAVING MONEY

A WORD OF CAUTION: WOMEN TEND TO PUT ALL THEIR WEIGHT ON PASSION

Women tend to want to follow the path they are most passionate about, even if nobody buys it or if it doesn't solve a major problem.

Don't make this mistake.

I want to caution you not to put all your financial future on your passion.

For instance, I'm passionate about bachata dancing and I'm good at it, too. If you don't know bachata dancing, it's similar to salsa, originates in the Dominican Republic, and is a bit more sensual.

Dancing comes very naturally to me, so while I have taught dancing in the past, I wouldn't say I excel at it because it comes so naturally to me.

However, I have a crazy great business mind. I love to teach it, my clients get incredible results, *and it's very profitable!*

Choose what you are most qualified to teach, what solves a major problem (so it creates a viable cash-flow-positive business), and what you are reasonably passionate about.

The richer you are, the more you can serve the world.

DOUBTING YOURSELF IS NORMAL

As you are reading this, you may have thoughts and doubts surfacing such as, "I can't guarantee **quantifiable end results.** So, how can I sell this?"

When you start getting into whether you can provide results, it's going to naturally bring up a lot of limiting beliefs, worthiness wounds, and things that make you feel unsure of your expertise.

Here's the number-one thing I need you to know right now: Every single person experiences this when they get specific on their high-ticket niche.

Everyone out there who's making a million, two million, five million, ten million, or more in their business was once where you are now, asking themselves if they are qualified enough yet to create a program that would result in these life-changing, tangible, quantifiable end results.

It is normal to have thoughts such as, *Oh, I could never promise they're going to lose weight,* or *I could never promise they're going to make more money,* or *I could never promise they're going to have the man of their dreams in their life.*

Every single coach out there who is an expert and honestly amazing at what they do has had the same thoughts you're having right now.

When the resistance comes up—and I promise you it will—*being of service* needs to be your motivator.

4

THE 3 S'S THAT MAKE AN IRRESISTIBLE OFFER

One decision can change your life forever.

—*Tony Robbins*

L ast month I had to take my baby to the vet. By my baby, I mean my seventy-pound rescue pit bull who cuddles like nobody's business.

He had an infection and the vet sent me home with some medicine in chewable pills.

Well, my boy would not touch that pill! I tried to mix it with his food and he'd eat ALL the food, but he'd figure out a way to leave that one pill in his food bowl!

Finally, knowing I needed to get this medicine in his body right away, I wrapped the medicine in something delicious, something his mouth waters for, so when I presented it, he gobbled it down before he even knew what was inside.

BUTTER MAKES EVERYTHING BETTER

When marketing your services, you must present your offer like you would medicine to your dog—wrap what he needs (the medicine) up in something he wants (butter)!

You want to sell your clients what they want (butter = the money, the relationship, the body, the tangible thing they believe is so yummy and delicious and will have the greatest impact on their happiness) and give them what they need (the medicine is your unique method of the deeper work required to make the lasting change).

What is it the one thing she thinks if she just fixes it'll solve her problem of unhappiness?

The butter is the marketing. You are presenting what she wants—to lose weight/feel good in her body, get into her dream relationship, grow her business so she can have more time with her kids. The medicine is your program—your method, which can be a combination of strategy (tangible) and reprogramming her limiting beliefs (intangible).

Your clients usually don't want the inner work, nor do they think the inner work is going to solve their problem.

Create a program that goes deep so it creates lasting change. But market the program so it speaks to their human superficial, fleshy, animalistic, carnal desires.

Sell them what they want and give them what they need.

THE WAY YOU PACKAGE YOUR OFFER IS 50% OF THE PERCEIVED VALUE OF YOUR OFFER

When you shift from dollars-per-hour thinking, you must understand how it not only serves you better as a business owner, but it also serves your client better to buy an end result, not your time.

Your coaching or consulting will help them achieve an end result more efficiently, faster than trying to do it alone, and without all the pain they might otherwise have to go through. You're going to help them skip steps, get there faster, and keep them accountable. This is the value of investing with a high-end expert mentor.

How you position yourself and how you talk about your high-ticket offer will determine how much you can charge and who takes you up on your offer.

If you don't already think of yourself as the go-to expert in your niche, you'll have trouble getting others to believe it. And if you can't describe in a sentence or two what end result you help your clients achieve, you'll have trouble enrolling clients into your high-ticket program.

You must accomplish 3 things:

1. Get SPECIFIC on what end result your clients can expect to achieve.

2. Position yourself as the expert who can provide a SOLUTION.

3. Make sure your audience truly wants what you offer. Are people SEARCHING for a solution to this problem already?

If your offer is not clear, it will be confusing and you won't be able to help anyone. If what you offer is too vague and no one understands exactly what ONE pain you can solve for them, you will be seen as a generalist, not a specialist, and certainly not an expert. People don't buy from generalists.

If your end result is not clear in your marketing, no one will understand why they should invest with you. This is critically important because...

CONFUSED OR UNCLEAR BUYERS DON'T BUY

The best way to describe what it is you do is by first defining your ideal client and what they want to achieve, mention the pain they want to avoid, and then apply your unique method. I learned this from 8-figure earner and master marketer Dan Henry. It works like this—you just fill in the blanks:

I help _____ (whom you serve)

get _____ (thing they want to achieve)

without _____ (thing they want to avoid)

by _____. (your unique method)

1. The first question is who do you help? Who are you specifically targeting? Women, men, entrepreneurs, female entrepreneurs, corporate women, moms? What's their age range? What's their lifestyle like?

2. The second part is: What do they want? Get specific here. This is the tangible end result. Bonus points if you use numbers.

3. The next part is the "without." This is key for creating your blue ocean, meaning how you stand out in the marketplace. What are some of the things your ideal clients do not want? Think about the old way of accomplishing their goal. Think about the objections they have to reaching their goal and the objections they have to the other pathways to achieve it. Are there methods that are common to your niche your clients already know about and may have already tried but failed? What do they want to avoid?

4. The last part is: What is it that makes you stand out in the marketplace? Describe your superior method of getting results.

My example of the refined marketing statement is as follows:

I help female experts create a 7-figure online business without doing low-ticket course launches and one-on-one sessions, by selling and scaling one high-ticket offer.

It doesn't mean I'm the only person in the world who does this. But I do stand out because I don't teach course launches, and I don't teach you how to build your business with one-on-one sessions.

My client is a smart and savvy buyer having already explored or failed at online courses or one-on-one sessions, and now she wants a new solution. I'm targeting a specific woman at a specific point in her journey.

So, you may want to ask yourself:

What has your ideal client already tried?

Is she in the beginning stages of her journey of getting to this end result?

Or is she savvy in the marketplace with lots of options?

Has she been researching this for years and knows the different pathways she could take?

Your marketing statement is not for your client, it's for you. In fact, you don't even have to share this marketing statement with anyone.

You know you help these specific people, *at a specific challenge point,* get this one thing without doing those other things they don't want to do by doing this proprietary thing you have created. Your evergreen webinar content is informed by this marketing statement.

The depth of your clarity here, the understanding of your ideal client's desires, and what they want to avoid, will in and of itself position you as the expert and allow you to command a high-ticket price.

MARKET RESEARCH

If you get stuck, the best thing you can do is market research. If you have an audience on Instagram or Facebook, you can start by asking the following questions in private and group conversations:

What's the biggest result you want to see right now in this area of your life?

What ways have you tried to solve this problem?

What hasn't worked?

What are you scared of about moving forward toward this goal?

What would make you doubt you can get results?

What way would you like to achieve this result?

What would be a dream come true as it relates to finding a solution to this problem?

5

CREATE A GREAT PROGRAM THAT GETS RESULTS FOR CLIENTS

Growth is never by mere chance; it is the result of forces working together.

—*James Cash Penney*

The best thing I did to grow my company was to develop a "method."

The key factor in capitalizing on this new opportunity in online education will be **creating a leading signature method or framework from your expertise**.

I know, I know, this feels like the most challenging part because you are a dynamic, multifaceted idea generator, and the task of fitting that into what feels like a "box" of ONE method or program makes you want to run.

I want you to know that in order to scale a business online sustainably, you must become known for something. This is what attracts high-level clients and allows you to increase profit margins.

Your marketing becomes less confusing and clearer for the world, which means greater impact on the people who need you. And you can systematize your business, which gives you more time for yourself and your family.

You develop one signature program and begin charging $5K for this program.

Every single woman who has something to teach can package up their skills into a high-ticket program and teach their clients on one group coaching call a week. This is how you can leverage your time, create greater profits, and get your clients to take their transformation seriously.

Once you have an overview of what you want to offer, map it out. What steps does someone need to go through from where they are to where they want to be?

You must plan out what the steps are to get from A to Z. You must teach them those steps and that's what your modules are about.

Think about the pathway, and what they should get plugged into on day one. What is the progression of the modules? What do they need for the whole program, and then what are the things they need to learn?

OUTLINE YOUR METHOD

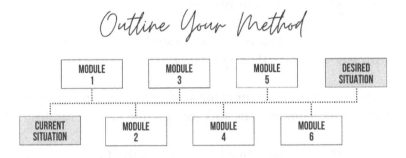

The main reason why someone buys a coaching program is to get an end result. They not only want the result, they also want it faster than someone who tries to do it alone. They want to buy a proven pathway from an expert: You.

You want to spend time outlining their journey from Point A to Point B, Current Situation to Desired Situation.

What markers need to happen to get them closer to achieving their Quantifiable End Result (QER)?

For our clients, it's what you're reading in this book: Choose Your Niche, Create Your Offer, Outline Your Program, Price the Program, Launch the Beta, Scale with an Evergreen Webinar. These milestones get 98 percent of our students to sell their first high-ticket program within twenty-eight days and build a seven-figure scalable business in ninety days.

Once you've mapped it out, you can start creating training modules. This is when you gather your intellectual property (IP) and build a curriculum around what you are teaching.

You can record videos of yourself teaching. These will be videos you can upload into a course hosting platform service like Kajabi, Teachable, or Clickfunnels to plug your students into when they enroll in your program.

This gives your students material to study apart from the time with you to answer their questions.

You'll want to include ongoing weekly calls to ensure clients gain momentum and are held accountable to their results.

What happens when you take the time to outline the curriculum, provide ongoing coaching support, and a community is that your clients get results quickly and they end up leaving you raving testimonials, which is awesome for your brand equity.

In fact, they will likely say it was the BEST investment in themselves they ever made and they wish they had done it sooner.

They will be ecstatic they paid you $5K, $10K, or even $50K.

THE CASE FOR GROUP COACHING

Clients get better results when they are amongst their peers. One of the best things you can do in your business is to facilitate group coaching. It not only gives you leverage so you only have one coaching call per week instead of ten, but it's also been proven that clients get better and faster results when they are held accountable in a group.

Group masterminds have proven to be the most effective way to create new habits and get quick results in the areas of a client's life or business that they want to change.

1. Exposure helps them see what's not in their experience. They will grow mentally, spiritually, and financially, just by being around others on a similar path. It's like osmosis learning.

2. It's way easier to not show up for yourself when no one sees you. You can slowly fade into the darkness and later people say, "Whatever happened to Sally?" But it's way harder when you feel seen and known in a group, when you know someone (or a group) is watching you, when someone is expecting results from you.

3. When we're in a group environment, we're beholden to show up for your group. It's not just about themselves, it's about showing up for others. Perhaps the thing that keeps us going some days is not our goals but supporting the other women in the community, and in those rough moments we give what we have to others, until we see the light again.

FEAR OF UNHAPPY CLIENTS

The women in our communities want to ensure their clients will get results. They are afraid of charging "too much" and then the client will be unhappy.

Here's the thing: Not every client will get the results they want.

Let me repeat: *Not every client will get the result THEY want.*

I've had a number of clients come back many months later and tell me they FINALLY got it. Your client may not get the tangible result they wanted in the timeframe they wanted. Don't make it about you.

Just check in with yourself: Have clients gotten results in the past? Did this client do all the work? As long as you have delivered the program and did everything you know to do to give them everything they need, then you did your part. It is a two-way street.

There is a variable in the process of your client's getting results, and that is THEM.

You can't do the work for them. They must be willing and committed to work through the hard moments, to actually follow the program especially when things get tough, to stay in the fire and believe in themselves.

That is something you can't guarantee.

Don't let this fear hold you back from walking forward powerfully to serve the people who are ready.

6

HOW TO STAND OUT IN A SATURATED COACHING MARKETPLACE

*"Stars do not pull each other down to be
more visible; they shine brighter."*

—*Matshona Dhliwayo*

When Sara Blakely founded SPANX, she didn't think, *There's no need for more pantyhose or leggings.* She didn't shy away from competing in a saturated marketplace. Instead, she found a problem she could solve within an existing industry, and now she owns a multi-billion-dollar enterprise.

Sara Blakely took advantage of a new opportunity in the marketplace. She noticed she could fulfill a need that wasn't being met yet. What was that need? Pantyhose that held everything in, smoothed everything out, and didn't roll down. Next-level pantyhose.

It's like when my client Beth came to me, she was already a master's level registered dietitian and a health coach, she was burned out on one-to-one sessions and selling a low-ticket course for barely $1,000 in sales each launch. She couldn't imagine how she could sell for a higher price.

After guiding her through the method I'm explaining in this chapter, we created her blue ocean by uncovering how she was different from every other health coach out there.

You see, Beth saw a problem in the diet industry. Most coaches and providers were telling women to use crazy diets and do extreme workouts. Beth had her own experience of why that method didn't work for her.

She learned to differentiate herself in the marketplace by teaching her new method. She shows women how to lose weight sustainably with intuitive eating, which allows her to resonate with a specific group of women and thus carve out her blue ocean.

She is passionate about intuitive eating. She believes in this deeply. She stands for this. And this is how she differentiates herself in a crowded market.

Of course, she's not the only health coach who stands for this and teaches this way, but she does differentiate herself from most of the diet industry.

You may look at the online coaching and consulting industry and think, *There's no space for me. Who needs another health coach?*

Let me ask you this: Is there a shortage of people who need help with weight gain, healthy eating, and terminal illness diagnosis?

Therefore, there is definitely a need for more experts in all niche categories.

What do you believe is needed in your chosen niche? What do you feel strongly about hardly anyone seems to be teaching? What are some secrets you'd like to expose? Or myths you'd like to bust?

This is how you carve out your blue ocean in a thriving industry.

7

STORY SELLS

"Content builds relationships. Relationships are built on trust. Trust builds revenue."

—Andrew Davis

What's important to remember is when you're coaching, you're usually helping people who are only five to ten steps behind you in your journey, and they want to get from where they are now (where you used to be) to where you are now.

If you can help them understand where *you* were and what *you* went through to get where you are now, it is incredibly powerful. It also connects them with you on a deeper emotional level. When they connect with the feeling "we've lived similar lives," they want to move closer to you. Your values, morals, and story all matter in the marketplace. When you share who you really are, your ideal client will be magnetized to you.

Your Buyer Wants to Know You

Think about the last ad for coaching you clicked on. I can almost guarantee there was some personal element in the copywriting or the video or image.

We are human and even when making logical decisions, it's more emotional than we think.

We want to work with someone we like. And we build this like factor in the marketplace by sharing who we are.

Studies show bland marketing, advertising, and webinars don't convert and perform as well as those with a unique personal brand, story, and a personal WHY.

When sharing your story, think about the most significant pieces that highlight the highs and lows.

The framework below can be used to share your life story, or a story that happened yesterday. It helps to highlight the important details that resonate emotionally with your buyer.

Part 1—Your Backstory

I grew up in a first-generation American household. There were the hardships of an alcoholic dad, a working-class family, and then a divorce.

My parents instilled a strong work ethic in my brother and me to find jobs that were secure and stable. My parents didn't get a higher education, so they wanted that for us.

I was the high achieving, Type A personality in college. I studied economics even though I hated it. I thought I could secure a financial future with that degree, so that's what I pursued.

I landed a job with the top hedge fund in the world right out of college. I moved on to a Fortune 50 company, working in Manhattan, making multiple six-figures per year.

Part 2—Your Burning Desire

What were the tangible things you thought would be the answer to your problems? What did you want?

I had all the stuff, yet I had these thoughts that *this can't be all there is to life*. I felt empty. There was no heart or meaning with my finance career path.

The pain surfaced, but I didn't know what to do about it.

I knew I didn't want to show up to a job every day and have someone else tell me what to do. I knew my desire was to have financial freedom and to become an entrepreneur. But I didn't have any idea what I was qualified for outside my current job. I felt stuck!

When you look at your story from your point of view today, you might be tempted to answer that your burning desire was self-love or self-care, or peace of mind. But *back then* you wanted something tangible—financial security, a career you love, to find a life partner.

Part 3—The Wall. At this point in your journey, you hit a wall. You think, *I don't know what to do now. I'm stuck. I can't find the answer. I'm really facing a hard time. I have a big problem. I don't know where to go to solve this problem.* You articulate this as part of your story. If you only have a few minutes, you can make it brief and to the point, like this:

> I hit a wall in 2009 when the financial crisis hit the country and I was laid off, along with thousands of others who lost their jobs. It felt like my life was coming apart and I had to find a solution fast.

Part 4—Your New Path

After you hit a wall, you have an epiphany, and it sets you on a new journey—the solution to your problems.

> After I lost my job, I did a lot of soul searching while I traveled all over the world. I decided to start an online coaching business from my little beachside house in Tulum, Mexico.

Part 5—The Challenges You Faced

After the epiphany, you come up with a plan, and as you follow the plan, you have some challenges. You run into some conflict, you have more challenges, and you struggle through hardships.

> When I was just starting out, I priced my first online course at $197. I had a list of about 200 people. I went through an exhausting ten-day "launch" period, trying to get women to join. After all my hard work and effort, four women joined.

> I was also exhausted at the thought of doing that again. And who else would buy? If the women who had already seen my offer didn't buy, then who would next time? I didn't know where to look for new prospects.

That means I made less than $800 in *revenue*, not profit. Because I likely worked over sixty hours to make that happen, I made about $13 per hour.

Ouch.

But hey, look on the bright side, right? Four women joined and it was my first course!

Problem was, what was I going to do to make money the next month to cover living expenses?

Questions and doubts started to fill my mind. Could this ever work?

Part 6—Your Total Transformation

Think about what happened to you and add that to your story. You saw the light, you broke through, you started to have some actual achievement, and then you had the total transformation.

I finally invested in some coaches, and they taught me how to build an actual online coaching business that works; I learned what I had to do every single day to make the business run like a company and not a hobby.

Now I have a three-million-dollar-a-year business selling one high-ticket coaching program. It is simple, effective, and profitable.

At the end of the day, people buy from you because they resonate with your story. If a prospective client must choose between Coach A and Coach B, they will choose the one they

LIKE the most—the one with whom they feel they could look out over the ocean, clinking champagne glasses.

You've got to share your story, not only to attract your ideal clients but also to help them see you're the ideal coach for them.

PART II

GOING TO MARKET

8

ARE YOU TESLA OR WALMART?

"In order to be irreplaceable one must always be different."

—*Coco Chanel*

I think Tesla did it right.

Instead of using a "trip-wire" model of offering a budget friendly car at $35K, they started with a "high-ticket" pricing model with their first car launching with an MSRP of around $100K.

The higher-priced car helped Tesla gain attention, exclusivity, and DESIRE. They started attracting a larger audience through the high barrier to entry of buying a Tesla.

Most people can't afford a $100K car. But some people CAN. And you know what that did?

Besides making the car an exclusive offer not everyone has the luxury of experiencing and thereby creating more desire, it gave them CASH FLOW to re-invest in perfecting the business and later building out other lower-tiered product lines to serve the market.

Rather than start with a low-priced offer to a small audience who doesn't even know they exist and end up failing with cash flow problems, they were able to secure their position with high profit margins and positive cash flow.

And just think, when Tesla started there was no shortage of luxury cars in the marketplace.

The management team could've thought, "There's no space for us" or "No one's going to buy a Tesla when they have Mercedes and Maserati" or "I can't charge that much since we're so new to the market."

But they didn't. What they did was create an amazing, irresistible offer that was a new opportunity in the marketplace.

They created a cutting edge, super-fast, 100% electric, self-driving, vegan-leather car people want.

They didn't shy away when people thought driving electric was a ridiculous idea.

They didn't quit when other competitors came on the market with their electric model.

Nope. They doubled down. They were able to innovate and differentiate themselves because of the elite business model they implemented from the beginning.

At the end of the day, it simply makes more sense to start high and then, if you want to, launch a lower-tiered offer once your business is established and has gained market share.

Your Business Cannot Survive Without Cash Flow

If you're struggling financially and your revenue numbers barely cover your expenses every month, there's nothing left over to re-invest back into the business. If that happens month after month, year after year, your business won't survive.

The number one thing a business needs, no matter what niche it's in, whether it's in the technology industry or it's a brick-and-mortar shop or restaurant, is cash flow. A business cannot survive without cash flow.

Studies show that the quicker any new business can come into positive cash flow, the higher the chances it will have of succeeding past the two-year mark.

Positive cash flow comes from higher profit margins and higher profit margins come from charging higher prices.

In this way, you can take a portion of your net income and keep reinvesting to grow not only your sales and revenue but also market share in your niche.

We've seen it time and time again, the reason one percent of the coaching and online education industry leaders make six figures or more per month, while 99 percent are struggling, is because they've built a solid structure from the beginning and gained market share by having the ability to spend more on advertising.

If your competitor has $25K to spend on advertising this month, and you have zero, who do you think will win in sales numbers?

Positive cash flow gives you the ability to re-invest in your business—and that includes advertising to reach more people.

Imagine if your business fails. If it doesn't become cash flow positive, you can't keep reinvesting in your business, which means you can't keep growing your business, you can't hire people, and you can't invest in advertising. You can't pour more money into the business if you're not making money in your business. Then all the people who are out there and need to be served by you and your business will not be served.

You have a responsibility to God's calling on your life, to yourself and your personal goals, to your family, and to all the people you feel called to serve to make sure you structure your business in a way that will succeed.

Not only that, but a high-ticket program is also the best possible way to guarantee your clients will have the accountability they need to ensure results. A win-win for everyone!

ARE YOU UNDERCHARGING AND OVER-DELIVERING?

Did you know women make up half the population, earn more than half of all undergraduate degrees and 60 percent of all master's degrees, but make up fewer than the top 10 percent of top earners and less than 5 percent of Fortune 500 CEOs? Why is that?

These women are highly educated. They're highly capable. But they're not represented in the business world. Most women have been conditioned from birth to behave in certain ways— to be quiet and not ask for what they want, to work tirelessly without pay, to not charge too much, to give freely without expectation of compensation.

No wonder women are underrepresented in the business sector!

When women begin to take up space in the coaching and online education world, they look around to see what other women are charging. Then, they base their pricing on what they see.

The problem is, most women are undercharging and over-working, so most women are basing their pricing on someone else's poverty consciousness.

Have you ever heard about the flea in a jar experiment? Researchers placed some fleas in a jar with an open lid, and they jumped out. Then, the researchers placed them back in the jar and capped the lid. Of course, the fleas would jump up and hit the lid, but after a while, the researchers removed the lid. This time, the fleas jumped only as high as if the lid were still there. The fleas were conditioned to fly only to the invisible ceiling.

Not to compare you to a flea, sis, but are you operating within an invisible ceiling on how much you can charge?

Experts who charge per hour for one-on-one sessions are trading their time for money. Even if they do eight sessions a day, five days a week, there is a cap on their income.

Doctors, lawyers, therapists, coaches, and consultants who charge $100 to $300 an hour are trading dollars for hours. These women may be the best of the best, but they are totally capped on how much they can make.

Running a business this way is exhausting.

Imagine needing to take a day or a week off. Your clients have developed a need for your time (they become codependent on your time instead of focusing on their results), so you feel like you can't take time off, or you feel guilty for needing it. You become a slave to your clients.

And on top of that, you don't get paid if you take time off, which means your livelihood is dependent on trading your time for money.

This is unsustainable.

What if your child gets sick? What if you aren't feeling well?

The other thing many women are doing when they come to us is selling a program for $397 or $997.

The problem with this, as mentioned earlier in this book, is that you need to have a very large following to get the kind of sales numbers you need to reach your goals. And once one launch is finished, you need to prep for the next one.

Listen: It is just as hard to sell a $197 product as it is to sell a $15K product.

Why? Because people buy results.

They don't buy downloads. They don't buy PDFs. They don't buy tactics. They buy SOLUTIONS to problems. People want HELP, not another download collecting cyber dust on their hard drive.

Why waste your time building another course that either won't sell or will collect dust on your client's hard drive? Why not give them what they really want? Instead of selling them a $197 product, sell them a $15,000 transformational program. Sell them the solution to their problem.

When you have a clear solution (end result), you can name your price because it's worth a hundred times that for your client.

9

DEVELOP "PROOF OF CONCEPT" (YOUR BETA OFFER)

"This philosophy teaches us to leave safe harbor for the rough seas of real-world experience, and to accept that a rough copy out in the world serves us far greater than a masterpiece sitting quietly on our shelves."

—*Chris Matakas*

Once you have clarity on your niche, high-ticket program, price, and offer, you will want to validate your offer by creating proof of concept. In the online coaching and consulting world, we do this by creating a beta program.

Do you start by spending hours and hours building out all the video training modules, worksheets, and assignments for your program? After all, you wouldn't feel confident selling something that wasn't even created yet, right?

Wrong!

Remember Beth? She had created her coaching program—the video modules, the worksheets, and all the other components—priced it at $197, and only three women bought it—less than $1,000 in sales!

She spent dozens of hours creating all the content, and then it flopped! So, she earned around $2 per hour for all the time and work she put into it.

Your beta is *key*. It's your trial run. It builds your confidence and gets you used to selling. But the key is to get paid *while* you create your program.

You must SELL before you create.

Well-constructed proof of concepts are designed to achieve the following four things:

1. Verify your solution solves a life transformational problem in the marketplace.

2. Confirm this solution is desired in the marketplace.

3. Determine whether people will pay for your solution.

4. Receive a quick cash flow injection.

How to roll out your beta:

1. Set your beta price at 50 percent off the price you will be charging in the future. For example, if your program is going to be $5K for a twelve-week group program (eight to twelve weeks is standard) when you fully roll it out to the masses, you would sell the beta for $2,500.

2. Decide how many people you'd like in your beta. If you have a very small audience and are launching your very first offer, a handful is a great number. Say you set a goal to have five people enroll (five to ten is ideal). 5 X $2,500 (beta price) = $12,500! Would you be happy with that for your first high-ticket beta program?

3. Create buzz around your beta program. To sell your beta, you should create a Facebook group and invite ideal prospects to join the group. You can do this by doing organic marketing: posting on social channels. Then you can schedule a live webinar training event in your Facebook group. Follow the webinar advice in Chapter 14, invite them to book a strategy call with you, and follow my sales training in the Chapter 11 of this book on every call.

Not only does a beta launch validate your high-ticket program (proof of concept) but it also gets you into positive cash flow. You now have money to invest in technology to help you automate your system, which is critical for scale.

10
SOCIAL PROOF

*"Repeat business or behavior can be
bribed. Loyalty has to be earned."*

—*Janet Robinson*

When's the last time you looked up a restaurant, bought something on Amazon, or investigated a salon or spa online? Did you check the reviews? Did you make your decision based on the number and quality of those reviews? Of course you did!

Social proof is everything. People read reviews before making purchases. It's become the norm.

You are discerning when you make a purchase, and your clients will be too.

The best thing you can give them is social proof. This provides a level of trust and comfort that you are who you say you are, you do what you say you do, and people have already gone through your program and gotten results.

Part of the reason why testimonials are so important is that they help create a deeper, more emotional appeal for your signature program.

As your reputation and expertise grow, your prospective students will see themselves more in your successful student's journey than in yours.

It also proves you can not only create results for yourself but you can also create powerful transformational containers for your clients. It also sets you apart from all the so-called "experts" who are popping up all over the place online.

Anyone can become a "marketer." A product seller can learn how to market their product to make money, but this doesn't guarantee quality, right?

Your prospects are thinking the same way. They won't just believe you. But they will believe the results you create.

When you sell the beta program, you will say, *"In exchange for the discount I'm offering for this beta round, I'm going to ask you for quality feedback so we can improve the program before we go out to the full marketplace. Will you do that?"*

Once your beta round is complete, you now have "proof of concept" and you know you have a solid program to market to future clients. Your beta run is an awesome time to get your first testimonials.

During the program run of eight to twelve weeks, you'll want to be keenly listening for questions and concerns they have. These point to gaps in the program content and delivery. Ask yourself, how can you fill these gaps?

Your ideal scenario is that each beta client gets incredible, life-changing results and they become RAVING fans. You will want to screenshot any wins inside your private student Facebook group, including the name of the group so it shows even more social proof this is in fact your program's testimonial.

You can also schedule a time to do a case study interview with them. On it you'll want to cover what they were experiencing BEFORE working with you, the doubts, fears, and skepticism they had, what they learned inside the program, and then the results they are now experiencing.

After the beta run, I highly suggest you set up a private chat with them directly so they can share any constructive feedback they have for you.

Finally, you will be able to use the testimonials in your full-blown evergreen webinar when you are ready to scale. Testimonials like these:

- My client Michelle just booked *$80,000 working with us inside High Ticket Empress!*
- My client Shelli just increased her income from *$500 a month to $5K a month* in just a few weeks, and she wasn't even sure this was possible for her because she is a beginner coach.
- My client Lisa has finally gotten total clarity and courage to *leave her multi-six-figure corporate C-Suite career of 20 years* and finally go full-time with her passion for helping other women break free...
- My client Rebecca just *sold her first $50K coaching package* (after only working with me for 8 short weeks) *and now has our automated webinar funnel working to bring her qualified leads who pay!*

- My client Alex has finally shifted her money mindset, implemented our high-ticket strategies, and is charging AND *enrolling at high-ticket prices—$3,500K per client for a $12K ROI within weeks.* This from charging $100/hour has changed her life and business.
- My long-time private student Tasha *just had a $33K month after we mapped out her path to a $1MM coaching empire.* From here, it won't be challenging scaling to $83K per month ($1M per year).
- My client Lilly just went from working her coaching business for over 3 years and still *never busting past the $10K mark and has finally hit $20K months and is holding her first LIVE event in 2021* (before this she had tried every single business fad out there and it made her life more complicated while never increasing her income).
- My client Emily went from *$0 to selling $8K relationship coaching packages,* filling her Costa Rica retreats, and enrolling students into her $20K/year Mastermind.
- My client Linda is so excited about her business because now she has a clear plan that WORKS and she knows exactly what to do every day to bring in income. *She sold over $12K in her beta program after struggling with $125 sessions.*
- My client Chelsea moved *from charging $125 per hour* as an embodiment teacher to a *high-end transformational coach for $2500 per package.* Her clients are raving about her and they are paying her more!

11

REIGNITING YOUR
LOVE OF SALES

"My life didn't please me, so I created my life."

—*Coco Chanel*

I f I heard "I need to talk to my husband" or "I need to think about it" one more time, I was going to quit.

In fact, I almost quit some years ago when it felt impossible to get people to say yes.

I loathed sales calls and wasn't very good at them, so I concluded this business wasn't for me.

Then I thought, I should just sell a low-ticket course so I never have to get on a sales call again.

That didn't work either.

One of the most beautiful things about building an online education and coaching company from your own expertise, gifts, and talents is how it will absolutely call you to expand in areas where your skills are weak.

You can either heed the call or turn away from it.

Ultimately, I decided not to be a quitter and to get better at the skill, and the good news is that selling high-end coaching is a learnable, trainable skill.

What I love about what I teach now is how 90 percent of the sale happens BEFORE the call. It's in the clarity of your niche and offer, the tangible, quantifiable end results in your big promise, and the sophistication of your messaging to handle your client's objections, all of which happens in the webinar funnel *before* the call.

For most people, selling is the scariest part of building their own business. And let's face it, if you don't get good at sales in a coaching business, or in any area of your life, it will cost you everything.

Let's look at the numbers to see why getting good at this is so important. If your current sales average $8K per month, and by improving your sales skills you double your monthly sales, you just went from $100K a year to $200K per year—just by getting better at sales!

If you sell for another twenty years at that same rate, you will make $2 million more. Start to think about this in lifetime value. If you know at this point you are going to sell for another twenty years before you decide you're not going to work anymore, whether you are selling your coaching program or something else, getting better at sales is huge. As an entrepreneur, you are always going to be selling something if you want to continue sharing your gifts.

Let's take the numbers higher. Let's say your sales are $500K per year or about $40K per month. If you double your sales just by increasing your sales conversions, then you are now earning $1 million a year without changing anything other than getting better at sales. The lifetime value of that is $20 million! Can you see why getting better at this skill is worth it?

Let's start at the baseline:

People hire a coach, specifically a high-ticket coach, because they have a current problem or need and they want a solution, and they have not been able to accomplish it on their own.

No one hires you because of your program—they don't hire you for your modules or a downloadable PDF. They hire you for a result. They are in pain and they need a solution. They have a situation they don't like and a desired situation they want.

They need to be experiencing a level of urgency around eliminating their discomfort. You'll want to tap into the drivers motivating your prospect to make a decision now, which can only be done by making the decision somewhat emotional.

The truth is people will stay in their current state of discomfort even though they don't want to. When you add EMOTIONAL URGENCY, this will elevate you, your prospects, and the quality of your candidates:

EMOTIONAL URGENCY + TRUTHFUL TIME/ AVAILABLE URGENCY = ACTION!

Here's what I want you to know. Sales *is* service. And high-ticket selling is how you not only transform your own life but also the lives of all the people you're going to touch through your high-ticket signature program.

We're going to get into the script, but first let's say a prayer. I highly suggest you take five minutes or more before a sales call to ask God to be with you through the conversation and that the highest and best outcome is revealed for both of you. Then release all attachments to the sale.

Dear God,

Allow me to make a heart connection with NAME. Help me to connect with her deeply and speak with love and clarity. Allow me to step into my power to serve this woman.

Thank you.

OUR MILLION-DOLLAR SALES SCRIPT

Pre-Phone Call: Your Marketing

The first step in the sales process needs to be your marketing. To powerfully invite prospects to a phone call, we invite them from a webinar they see displayed on ads we run. This is all set up and automated; it's running around the clock.

Step One: Bonding

Your client is buying from YOU. If they don't feel connected to you, they won't buy from you.

What are your favorite personal words to bond?

Location: *Where are you Zooming in from today?*

Family: *Do you have kids?*

Feeling: *How are you feeling today?*

Step Two: Set the Agenda and Buying Atmosphere

Take the lead. Let your client know how the call is going to go.

Well NAME, what we've found works best on these calls is starting off with a deep dive into your current situation, including what's working, what's not working, and we'll go from there into where you want to be, your grand vision for your business, and where you want to take it.

And quite simply, if we determine we can help you close the gap between where you are right now, and where you want to be, then I'll absolutely show you how and what that process looks like. Sound good?

Step Three: Pain Diagnostic

Imagine you're a doctor and a patient comes into the exam room. They say they are experiencing some pain but it's not clearly visible where the problem is. The doctor will poke and prod and ask very directly: Does it hurt here? How about here? What about this? Did you try this?

So NAME, what motivated you to book the call with us today?

If I get the "gold awesome..." Gold is:

I'm struggling with doing all the things you said in the webinar/ on your post/in your video and I want to have a solution and I just don't know what to do. It sounds like you have a system that works well and I need help.

If you didn't get the gold, dig deeper. Ask again another way.

Keep asking question until you have a clear understanding of their physical pain, emotional pain, spiritual pain, what they've tried to do to fix it, and what they're missing out on because of it.

Step Four: Vision

ENERGY SHIFT away from Diagnostic and more into Encouragement.

The next step is to go into their vision. Most people are playing small and not allowing themselves to realize the significance of who they are and what they could be.

Okay gotcha, so to be super clear on what's going on here NAME... so let's jump ahead into where you want to go, where you want to be.

Let's say, NAME, we invite you into the program and Tara and her team show you how to do it:

*How to learn our new opportunity/pathway and how to implement a **simple 4-step process to get your DESIRED RESULT** that took me (and clients) from PAIN to RESULT.*

Let's say that you've implemented this 4-step method and you're seeing results in your BUSINESS/BODY/RELATIONSHIP.

What does this turn into for you, as an IDEAL GOAL?

You're looking for tangible specifics here, such as the following:

- Actual numbers in income
- Numbers in weight loss
- Pain going from an 8 to a 3 on a scale from 1–10
- Single to Married

Step Five: Intervene

Okay NAME, so you're currently in PAIN and you want to get to DESIRED GOAL.

Tell me, how soon are you looking to start experiencing DESIRED GOAL?

Answer should be ASAP!

Do you have a grasp right now on what's stopping you from achieving these results on your own?

Since you know yourself best, what tools or resources do you need to make this a reality?

Listen carefully for three magic statements before moving forward:

- Inability to do it on their own.
- Wanting to do it faster.
- Wanting to follow a proven system and have guidance by somebody who has done it.

Step Six: Invitation

Okay NAME, so based on the fact we're on the same page about everything, where you're coming from, and where you want to go, how committed you are to getting there, I am 100% confident we can help you. You are totally on the right phone call.

Your search for the coach, the mentor that's going to help you get to the next level, I know for you the search is over.

Would you like me to tell you about the PROGRAM NAME?

Step Seven: Confidently Close

When the prospect asks, you confidently tell them the investment to work with you. Remember, this is not a price, or a cost, it's an *investment*. You may offer them a discount to move forward on the phone. This is just a way to give a bonus to move past the fear that will inevitably be there. Remain silent while your client decides.

If your client has questions, also called objections, you will want to handle them succinctly, confidently, and with love. This is when YOUR confidence gets called into action. You must remain the leader and hold space for your prospect's fear and indecision.

Finally take the payment. Do your client a favor, and don't let them off the phone to "think about it." The reality is they already know if it's a yes or a no. Take the payment over the phone using a merchant account that processes credit cards.

I've developed a high-ticket sales cheat sheet for you. You can find it in the bonus resources.

To scale up, which we'll cover in the next part, you need to be able to step out of doing sales calls. You'll want to hire sales closers to take these calls for you. The idea is you can move out of sales and operations so you can focus solely on your "genius zone" of helping your clients reach their goals.

Because I'm able to step out of front-end sales and operations, I've been able to achieve milestones I never experienced before when I ran my business by myself. To date, we've hit $250K months, $80K weeks, and $30K days—and you can too!

PART III

Scaling Your Offer

12

YOU CAN'T LEAVE YOUR BUSINESS UP TO HOW YOU FEEL

*"The chief temptation that meets the soul and
assaults at every step of the pathway is feelings.*

—*Hannah Whitall Smith*

Out of nowhere, our sales had slowed down.

At first glance, I was anxious and worried, thinking
my ads weren't working. Then I thought, *maybe the
webinar isn't working anymore.*

I knew something was off, but I didn't know what.

After looking at my numbers—my click-through rates, con-
version rates, cost per lead, cost per call—I found everything
on that end was working incredibly well.

That's when the data uncovered the real problem: A sales rep
had stopped performing.

If I didn't have a system in place with numbers I could look at, I might have reacted in fear. Had I made choices based on *feelings* instead of *data*, I could have slowed sales even more. Instead, I was able to see the real problem, and I could fix it swiftly.

As women, we are emotional creatures. It's part of our beauty. But if you're leaving your business success up to how you FEEL, it will fail.

Think about it. When you leave your business up to how you feel, you have to be feeling good, creative, motivated, inspired, spacious, and have high energy, and you must be feeling all this consistently. But how many of us can continuously feel this way day in and day out?

The reality is your business requires consistency. You need incoming clients and continual cash flow. If your business requires manual work to create these, you are setting yourself up for failure.

What am I talking about when I say manual work? It's so many things—the daily post writing, video creation, participating in social media, and so many others. All these things are awesome! And yes, you should do them to build relationships with prospects and grow your community around your work.

But do you have the time and energy to do those things daily to hope and pray you get a client? When will you have time to be a wife, mother, get workouts in, and generally live your life? How are you ever supposed to succeed in doing those things manually when there are only so many hours in a day?

Take a deep breath and stop being so hard on yourself. I'll let you in on my secret to having consistent cash flow—you *must* have systems. Systems are the antidote to leaving your business up to how you feel.

Systems create data.

Basing business decisions or fixing business problems from your emotions is sure to fail.

We tend to catastrophize everything.

Numbers and data keep it real. When a problem arises, you look at the data and find solutions based on the data. When you don't have data to look at, you can't find the problem, and you end up trying to fix problems that aren't there.

Organic traffic doesn't give you data. Until you start a methodical system, you won't have data to look at.

When it comes to funnels and ads, the answers are in the numbers, not your emotions. I'll say it again: If you're leaving your business up to how you *feel*, it will fail.

Most coaches fail in the first two years of business. Think about it. It's because they don't become cash flow positive quickly.

If you don't have a system that brings you *inbound* clients, leads, people who will pay you, then you're setting yourself up for failure.

We speak with women every day who are interested in learning from us in High Ticket Empress, and they are running their business on organic traffic alone: doing a post and hoping and praying they'll get in front of someone who will want to work with them.

Obviously, I'm an advocate of paid advertising. I don't think you need this initially, but you do need to get automated ASAP.

This is a way you can warm up a cold audience to you when you're sleeping, when you're working out, when you're on vacation, when you're homeschooling your kids.

This is the beauty of technology.

If you don't have a system like this, then you are leaving your business up to how you feel. Meaning you have to *feel good*.

This is a huge risk. And frankly, history tells us already that we are moody, emotional, hormonal creatures, and if you consciously know this, then it means you are choosing to FAIL. Harsh? Yes, but also true.

You're not going to feel like going out and finding new people every day to keep cash flow going. You can't grow like that. You will stay stagnant.

And you can't leverage yourself because there's only one of you. You have to multiply yourself. You've got to employ something or someone to multiply you.

My automated masterclass brings us inbound leads every day. I recorded it once and it gets me and my expertise in front of hundreds of ideal people day in and day out.

This takes *me* out of looking for clients by using technology.

I have one high-ticket offer and one funnel. This creates a system—a scalable system.

If your idea of client generation is "giving free value" on Instagram, Facebook, and YouTube, then let's be honest— you're running your business like an amateur.

The two things that prevent coaches from scaling are the following:

1. Not enough cash flow.

2. Not enough eyes on your offer.

Having an online sales funnel that *converts* is now a critical asset for any coaching business.

The reality is that if you don't have a reliable way to attract premium prospects on autopilot, then your client lead generation is up to how you *feel*.

And let's face it, sister, how many days are you just plain exhausted from the hustle? Especially if you don't see results in the form of converted clients and cash?

The good news is that you only need to implement just one simple three-step funnel—it literally runs while you're sleeping or spending time with their kiddos—and it generates quality high-ticket client applications every day.

This is how you solve the scaling problem:

1. Create *one* premium offer with rolling enrollment.

2. Set up *one* three-step funnel that gets more eyes on your funnel.

Once you have your system set up, it's easier and simpler than you think to get past that $10K per month mark. In fact, you can scale to $100K months and beyond. This is the path to becoming a 7-Figure Coach.

13

HOW WE TRIPLED PROFITS

*Deliberately Seek The Company Of People Who Influence
You To Think And Act On Building The Life You Desire."*

—Napoleon Hill

Remember Beth, my High Ticket Empress client? She said the worst part of her "failed" launch of her $197 DIY online course was not the low sales numbers but the lack of follow through in her students.

They didn't watch all of her material, do the work, or get results.

They bought her course and she sent them away hoping they would watch the videos. To this day she doesn't even know if they completed the course.

It didn't fulfill the part of her that wanted to be of service, because she didn't see them all the way through.

When she started following the model I teach, she wasn't sure if the high-ticket group coaching model would work for her.

She had spent years doing one-on-one sessions, and she didn't know if her clients would feel safe to be vulnerable in a group space.

She was also concerned about her own ability to lead. It was one thing to be the leader of a one-on-one call, but being the leader of a group of ten or twelve made her feel insecure all over again.

Once she started reading clinical statistics of why and how clients get better results when they are among their peers, she decided to go for it.

Now she leads one coaching call a week with her high-ticket group coaching clients.

Taking the Hybrid Path

Transitioning from one-on-one into one-to-many is the paramount way you can remove a cap on your income. There are only so many one-on-one sessions you can do per day or per week. But you can theoretically serve dozens of clients on one two-hour coaching call per week.

Your students and clients start to shift out of the mindset they are paying for your time, and instead they are paying for a result. They take their participation seriously because people who *pay* also pay attention.

There are three main online education facilitation models:

DIY: Do It Yourself (Online Course)

This model is the low-ticket course model. You record a bunch of videos, sell course access, and let your student watch the videos and implement on their own time with no live coaching.

D4Y: Done-4-You

As a provider, you implement the deliverables for the client. This is usually sold at a very high premium. Not all niches can offer done-4-you. For example, weight loss can't be done-4-you.

DWY: Done with You (High-Ticket Coaching Programs)

This model is a hybrid and the one I recommend. You develop a method and create pre-recorded videos your students can watch "on demand" at any time. You also provide a live component whereby there are weekly or multiple weekly Q&A calls per week to help facilitate accountability and personalized feedback for each student.

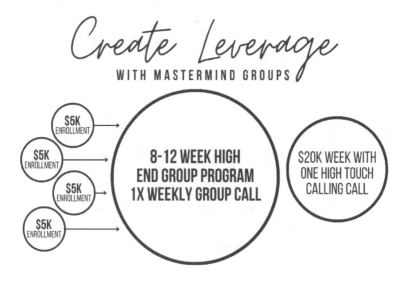

Create Leverage

WITH MASTERMIND GROUPS

$5K ENROLLMENT

$5K ENROLLMENT

$5K ENROLLMENT

$5K ENROLLMENT

8-12 WEEK HIGH END GROUP PROGRAM 1X WEEKLY GROUP CALL

$20K WEEK WITH ONE HIGH TOUCH CALLING CALL

Rolling Enrollment

A failed launch is excruciatingly painful.

The idea is you work crazy hard for ten days to launch a course starting and ending on a certain date. It's a mad rush to get as many people in before the "doors close."

The problem is, if you don't get as many as you wanted, if you don't hit your target numbers, there's nothing you can do.

You have to start the course on the start date, even if only two people enroll.

Ouch.

The antidote is rolling enrollment.

Not only does it solve the problem for you so you NEVER have to launch again, but we've found it's much better for our client results.

Think about it: Your new client is joining a group energy that is already established, which means they are walking into a party at 11 pm. It's rocking and rolling. There are people singing and dancing, someone is pouring drinks, someone who knows where the bathroom is, etc. You start vibing quickly because the energy is already there.

It's the same with your clients. They are walking into a group setting where people already know the lay of the land, they've had success, they've faced challenges, and they are happy to show the way to someone new. In fact, the ones who have been around for a while really love feeling like an expert in your program.

Your new client feels warmly welcomed. That new client joins four or forty or a hundred clients who are already inside. They jump in and feel called to do the work and catch up to the others.

The Q&A calls with you are there to answer everyone's questions no matter if it's their first or twelfth week in the program. This allows all students to learn from each other's questions.

Creating a premium group program with an automated lead generation system whereby clients can "roll" in at any time is the fastest, easiest, and most profitable way to scale.

On-Demand Training

CLIENTS → ON-DEMAND TRAINING

CLIENTS LEARN WHAT TO DO & HOW TO DO IT

WEEKLY COACHING CALLS/Q&A — YOU HELP THEM DO IT

PRIVATE COMMUNITY FOR SUPPORT — CLIENTS HELP EACH OTHER

14

THE SECRET TO SCALE IS IN THE SUBTRACTION

All things are difficult before they are easy.

—*Thomas Fuller*

When it comes to scaling to $1 million, it's not rocket science. It's way simpler than you think.

Instead of *adding* a million shiny objects, new programs, launches, low-ticket courses, podcasts, speaking, blogging, JV partners, live events, the gold is in the *subtraction*.

The most difficult part of scaling is staying focused and *not* adding, but in fact *subtracting*. It requires you to let go of all the new ideas you get daily and *go all-in on one path*.

Become known for one program and build an evergreen system to scale this one program. Evergreen just means that instead of launching, you have a dishwasher, washer-dryer, and refrigerator doing the work for you 24/7.

Ads and one epic webinar funnel can work as a 24/7 sales team.

Early in my online marketing and coaching career, I learned all the digital marketing tricks—profit ladders, funnels, upsells, downsells, tripwires, you name it.

It made logical sense to give away something for free, then add on a $97 product, downsell to a $27 PDF, upsell to a $297 course, and eventually a $1,997 course. The logic being it's easier to sell something at the lower price point than at a premium.

Well, I'll make a long story short and tell you it didn't work for me. I was spending all my time building fancy funnels and not doing my genius work with the people I wanted to serve.

I learned how the real secret of scale is LEVERAGE. To create leverage you need to simplify, automate, and streamline.

Here's how the top 1 percent of leaders in the online coaching, consulting, and education space are doing it:

1) Create one signature high-end product/program.

2) Teach one to many instead of one-on-one.

3) Automate lead generation—this removes YOU from the manual work of trying to find clients. The automation is evergreen and happening 24/7 while you sleep.

The steps above package up your expertise into one program to create the most impact. The delivery of this one program requires you to face your clients only one to two times per week in a group coaching call. Automated lead generation means once the setup work is done, creating a pipeline of new clients no longer requires hours and hours per day.

No one wants to work 24/7. In fact, you likely don't even want to be tied to your office desk forty hours a week. As a six-figure-a-month earner, I only show up to *two* coaching calls a week: One for High Ticket Empress and one for my Mastermind. You too can have this time freedom.

Freedom to spend your time how YOU want to. Freedom to be with your kids, to buy the clothes you want, the car you want, the house you want, to take the vacations you want when you want. Attaining financial freedom changes everything.

Automate Lead Generation—Our 3 Step Funnel

Clients of mine, a husband-and-wife couple, have 12,000 followers on their YouTube channel and a multiple six-figure-per-year online relationship coaching business, but when this couple came to me, they were exhausted from the launch model.

Their program investment was $6K, so they only needed seventeen new clients in one launch period for a $100K sales revenue launch. That sounds great until you realize how much work it takes to launch.

Launch periods are usually about ten days, meaning it's always incredibly intense to get as many people enrolled in this period as possible because once the "cart is closed," that's it. You have to accept whatever numbers you get.

During each launch they were doing dozens of sales calls, communicating with their joint venture (JV) partners, writing copy for emails, working with JV partners, doing videos for YouTube, posting everywhere online, AND serving their current clients!

Talk about intense!

And they were doing not one but *four* launches per year—for the last five years—making on average about $400K a year. They felt successful, but they were not set up to scale because the business was dependent solely on them.

Every piece of the business required them to work around the clock, which turned into a big problem because they hit a limit on how much they could make when all of the work relied on them.

They felt like they would just end a launch and then they had to start another launch. It felt like an up-and-down roller coaster instead of a steady machine creating leverage.

Their dream was to create an automated marketing and sales machine so they could focus on their genius zone of getting their clients incredible and fast results.

They saw how my business runs and knew they needed to set up an *evergreen* webinar and rolling enrollment for their program.

What is an evergreen system?

In **marketing**, the term **evergreen** refers to the products, segments, and strategies that stay relevant over a long period of time.

Instead of always creating a new course or a new webinar training, you make your webinar relatively timeless—meaning it solves a problem that's not likely to go away any time soon—and you set up evergreen marketing.

You create it ONCE, and people benefit from it for weeks, months, or even years.

For this couple, setting up an evergreen sales machine would accomplish three main things:

1) Take them out of the launch marketing exhaustion because they would have constant leads coming in 24/7/365.

2) Take them out of handling the sales calls because they would have a proven offer and already had over six figures in sales, which means they could hire sales reps to enroll new students.

3) They would be able to focus on delivery only and making their product best-in-class, placing all new students into a rolling group, which then would only require them to host one group coaching call a week.

Just from those three things we expect they will be able to massively improve profit margins, reduce the amount of hours they are working, and quickly scale to $2+ million per year.

Scaling a business requires taking yourself OUT of the business. Not entirely, but once you hit six+ figures in sales, the cash overflow needs to be used to automate and delegate, which leaves you more free time to focus solely on your genius zone of leading the vision of the company and the coaching or consulting expertise for client fulfillment, and spending time with your family and having an epic life!

This coaching duo took five years to discover the genius of an evergreen rolling enrollment system, but you can start out with it from the beginning!

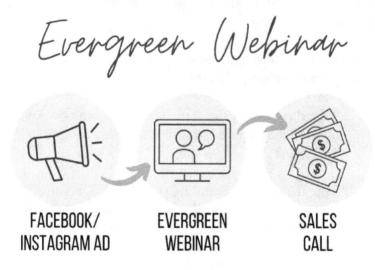

Evergreen Webinar

| FACEBOOK/ INSTAGRAM AD | EVERGREEN WEBINAR | SALES CALL |

Leverage Paid Advertising

Once you're at the point in your business when you have a solid offer and proof of concept your offer sells, you can sell it on a sales call, and your clients are happy with delivery and results, then it's time to pour some high-octane fuel on the fire!

Instead of manually posting new content every day, why wouldn't you pay for a system to post *for you*? Makes total sense, right?

Just like those big billboards you see along the freeway, companies with positive cash flow have advertising budgets. This helps ensure they keep driving sales.

You need to do the same with your online expert business.

I've already convinced you why you should charge higher prices, right? After all, your business won't survive if it doesn't have positive cash flow, and high-ticket offers is the way to get there as quickly as possible.

If you charge higher prices, you're able to invest a portion of your profit margins into advertising, thereby making future sales relatively certain, meaning you leverage your own time with an automated system.

One day I stood in my small home office and recorded a one-minute, forty-second video. That video was made into an ad for Facebook and Instagram. It has since brought us over $440K in sales.

Yes, that's what I said: One video I created holding my iPhone in my hand while standing in my small home office has generated over $440K in just a sixty-day period.

Let me break down for you how this works, and how it can work for you, too:

Let's say you spend $50 a day on ads, and 300 people watch your webinar over a thirty-day period. And let's assume about ten people opt-in per day—your stats may be different depending on a bunch of variables.

Generally speaking, 5 percent of those webinar viewers will take the call to action and book a call with you. And 20 percent of those people will buy and become clients.

Example:

500 conversions from one ad X 5% = 25 calls booked (30 days).
25 X 20% = 5 Clients
5 Clients @ $5K = $25,000 (sales)

Would you spend $5,000 to make $25K? Assuming a sale price of $5K, you just netted $20,000 for that month.

Now you can reinvest a portion of that revenue to double your ads budget, which could double your sales.

$10K in ad spend could become $50K in sales for the month.

Investing in paid advertising gives you data relying on organic traffic sources doesn't give you. Having data gives you power. You can easily see what's working, what's not working, where to double down, and where to lighten up.

PUT YOUR EVERGREEN WEBINAR ON AUTOPILOT

"Back in the day," a webinar was a networking event with a sales presentation. You know, there's a guy or gal at the front of the room selling you something and at the end you run to the back of the room to sign up.

Well, now we create all this with virtual technology.

Webinars build the know, like, and trust factors fast, and it also indoctrinates your prospect into your new opportunity in the marketplace.

When done well, the prospect knows by the end they want to work with you.

We all get how clients need to know, like, and trust you before they buy. Most coaches and experts are doing this process manually. They are manually posting all over social media hoping the algorithm works in their favor.

These organic traffic methods all work. BUT—and this is a BIG BUT—they require manual work, which requires manual time.

Again, remember the "trading hours for dollars" concept? We need to get out of that in all areas of the business.

If your model REQUIRES your time day in and day out, there is no leverage.

To get you out of relying on this method for client generation, automating an epic piece of marketing is the best way to do this. The most proven pathway is a webinar.

Maybe you've already tried crafting a webinar and it flopped. Or maybe it resonated and converted well with your prospects. In any case, webinars are still the best way to indoctrinate your prospects (cold leads) into your program and share your expertise—all on autopilot.

However, not all webinars are created equal. I can't tell you how many conversations we have with prospects for High Ticket Empress who tell us they created a webinar and it didn't work, so now they think webinars don't work. Honestly, it's not that webinars don't work, it's that *their* webinar, the webinar they created, didn't work.

I'm going to give you a framework for an epic webinar. But first, a little disclaimer: You must be clear on your niche and your new opportunity in the marketplace (Part I of this book). It must solve a major problem for someone; otherwise, it will land flat, meaning no one will turn into a client.

1) Make a BOLD promise. You're going to teach just ONE main concept.

2) Share your story—why do you care?

3) Share three secrets to solve their problem (break and rebuild their limiting beliefs).

    a) Secret #1: Teach the ONE thing: Why Your New Method Works Over the Old Way.

    b) Secret #2: Handle Their First Objection to Your New Method.

    c) Secret #3: Handle Their Second Objection to Your New Method.

4) Include testimonials to showcase results.

5) Powerful Call-to-Action (book a call).

If you don't craft and create your content in a way that 1) helps you stand out from other coaches who do the same as you, and 2) handles their objections to your method, then your webinar training won't turn into more clients or more cash.

HIGH-TICKET SELLING STARTS WITH RECEIVING

Everything in life requires an ASK—getting into the relationship you want, getting the career you want, getting the body you want—but asking is hard if you have issues with receiving.

Here's the hard truth: If you aren't available for true receiving, you won't succeed in any type of selling.

I want to share this with you because I know from experience how once you intellectually understand how it might be hard for you, then you can get better at it. It's exciting because if you acknowledge you want to get better at this, then you can.

You might think about going back to a job where someone else pays you, but you know deep down that's not even possible for you anymore because you know your potential and it's not going to make you happy.

Getting to be a pro at sales calls takes practice. I recommend getting a buddy to practice with you. In High Ticket Empress, I get students to hook up with each other so they can practice sales calls together while they are also getting on sales calls with clients. You have to practice sales calls to get better at it, just like you do with anything else.

And here's the reality: Your revenue in coaching is determined by the number of sales calls you are doing. Believe me, even though I have people who are doing these calls for me now, I still had to master them first.

Even if you get a sales team to do sales calls, you need to have a solid sales foundation. You need to believe in your product and its value to your potential clients. Your sales are a reflection of what you believe you deserve. The beauty is that you can shift this very quickly by following the sales strategy outlined in Chapter 11.

15

7 FIGURES AND BEYOND

"If people aren't calling you crazy, you aren't thinking big enough."

—*Richard Branson*

You might be wondering how you can scale without working harder. Well, the key is to take yourself out of the business.

Now, I know you might be thinking, this business is my baby! I don't want to take myself out of the business. What I mean is, *take yourself out of every aspect of the business that is not your genius zone.*

For me, writing this book is a key part of delivering on God's calling on my life, and if I didn't have a sales team, a coaching team, an ads team, a finance team, an executive assistant, and a home assistant, I wouldn't have the space to write this book.

The key is delegation and automation!

And you can't do either of those without setting your business up so pieces of your business can be automated and delegated.

The leverage you put in place allows you to remove yourself from the business—the admin, the finances, the sales, the media buying—and keep yourself in your genius zone.

How do you replace yourself?

I advise you start to look at your business in the following four quadrants:

Revenue: Products/Services (your High-Ticket Signature Program).

Traffic: Media Buying & Analytics (Paid Advertising).

Sales: Sales Manager, Sales Reps, and Sales Setters.

Ops/Legal/Finance: EA, VAs, Operations Manager, Onboarding, Training, Customer Support, Bookkeeping, CFO, Financial Advisors, Taxes.

I want you to start thinking of yourself as a CEO and then contemplate the three things that take most of your time.

As the CEO, your primary role is to focus on the vision of the company and drive it forward. However, most CEOs get caught in the weeds for way too long.

The "how" doesn't get you to scale past the million-dollar mark, it's the "who."

The first thing I did when I began selling my first few high-ticket programs was set up a paid advertising webinar funnel to automate our client lead generation. I went from being petrified to speak on camera, on stage, into a mic, and recording myself on webinars to loving the funnel system.

The second thing I did when I hit $50K a month was to hire my first salesperson, then two, then three. You can't scale your expert business if you are both selling and delivering the program.

The third thing I did was to hire assistant coaches to help me with client delivery and fulfillment. It is very important to me that every client of ours feel seen and heard and get all the personalized coaching they need. I love coaching, so I still have one coaching call a week, but High Ticket Empress offers three calls a week to provide our students with a lot of support.

Our High Ticket Empress coaches have gone through the High Ticket Empress program and are certified in our method. These coaches now host additional coaching calls per week for our students.

I now have an executive assistant, and we have a social media team to cover Instagram, YouTube, and Facebook content and community management.

In general, I work no more than twenty hours per week, and usually take three-day weekends! I tell you this because I want you to see the vision. Getting to a million or more per year in your online expert business does not mean you have to work all the time, sacrifice being a mom or being a wife, or lose your mental and physical health in the process.

Upsells

As I've scaled High Ticket Empress to $250,000 in sales per month, it has naturally created demand for a higher-level mastermind program.

My Mastermind program is available to be upsold to a certain small percentage of high achievers in High Ticket Empress who want more access to me so they can scale even quicker.

In the Mastermind, I host three coaching calls per month, and three in-person live events per year, and the investment is four times higher than HTE.

An upsell mastermind like this can add $750,000–$1,500,000 in revenue per year to your business.

PART IV

7-Figure Heart

16

YOUR HEART IS THE DRIVER

*"We cannot create a new future, by holding
on to the emotions of the past."*

—Dr. Joe Dispenza

My dad would come stumbling up the back deck steps. You could cut the tension in the house with a knife because he was late and my mom, brother, and I already knew what it meant.

He was probably drunk.

He'd be riddled with guilt, and it would be obvious from his wrinkled forehead.

I would try to ease the tension between my parents so we wouldn't have to experience another fight. My brother would retreat to his room to avoid it all, and I would stay and "run point" for my parents, trying to ease tensions, stepping up to adulthood at just five years old.

My dad had an alcohol addiction and honestly, bless his heart. He was a very sweet man. He passed three years ago at age sixty-three from alcohol abuse.

Psychologists would say I'm a parentified child and there's long-lasting effects to having this experience early in life.

If you didn't have parents who were highly attuned to you and your needs and your feeling of safety, or were caught up in their own drama, then your nervous system may be jacked up.

Are we going to be fed on time? Is he going to come home drunk again? Is there going to be a fight? These were all the things I was tracking starting at age four, and that's not something a child should even be thinking about.

I share this with you because a lot of people, and me included, used to think trauma meant something like physical or sexual abuse, but that's not true. Those are real traumas, but emotional traumas are also legitimate and have long-lasting, often hidden effects on your adulthood.

I grew up in suburban Connecticut and went to private school. We always had food on the table. I had nice clothes. I did all the extracurricular activities like dance, piano, gymnastics, softball, and so on. We had a comfortable house in a safe neighborhood. Despite all that, there was trauma.

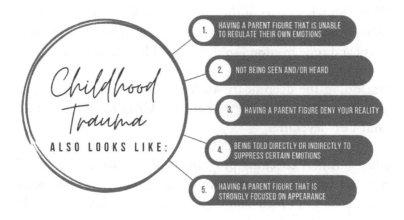

THE DEPTHS OF YOUR ROOTS

I had built a half-a-million-dollar business, but then I burned out, and almost burned everything down.

I really didn't understand what was happening at the time. What I discovered through my healing journey is how I had a lot of heart wounds that were running in the background, and I was totally bypassing them.

I was using mindset (intellectual) or spiritual work (energetic) to completely bypass the damaged neural pathways in my heart and nervous system.

This is what I see as an epidemic in the personal development and spiritual development world. So many of us are bypassing our emotional realities. It's a bad thing because it always catches up with us eventually. And we can't sustain the growth, the success, and the wealth we're striving for.

Remember how I told you that you must sell your client what they want and give them what they need?

Well, this whole part of the book is a perfect example of this. Women want to be able to stand on their own feet with flexibility and time freedom, so that's how I lead in my marketing.

But doing the deep heart work is what I must give you so you actually become the woman who CAN receive and hold your next-level life.

Most business coaching programs will give you strategy and mindset work, but they are missing the work on your heart that causes you to self-sabotage, self-abandon, and play small.

Your capacity to hold more wealth and responsibility has everything to do with the health of your heart. The height of your tree can only go as deep as your roots.

Your Nervous System

Constant overthinking, analyzing, and intellectualization is a form of dissociation from the body. It is a survival tactic that only gets us so far because ultimately dissociation causes disconnection and a stunting of emotional maturity as we grow up.

The sympathetic part of the autonomic nervous system, which regulates flight or fight, is on high alert when real or perceived danger is imminent. This system prepares the body to cope with stress and threats, as well as returning the body to a resting state afterward (the parasympathetic nervous system). If your body doesn't self-regulate well, you may be living in a constant state of stress.

Your nervous system is always working for you, not only with current real-time events but will also send your body into fight/

flight mode when you are triggered because of an event from when you were a child, like the five-year-old me.

The heart is the sensory organ that guides our decision-making ability as well as our understanding of ourselves and our place in the world. If our heart is broken from early in life, it will have lasting affects not only on our physical health, but our mental and emotional health, thereby holding us back from reaching our full potential.

If your body is still operating in survival mode from early trauma, you will function from an animalistic, primitive response rather than from the higher, heart-centered emotions.

But just like anything else, you can learn how to heal your heart and nervous system by first understanding intellectually what happened to you and the behaviors you now engage in to try to protect yourself, and then learning embodiment practices to move all the stuck and stagnant energy out of your body.

You can learn and increase your resilience, which is the capacity to process, integrate, regulate, and bounce back after trauma or triggers that surface past traumas.

Early childhood trauma changes your brain, and it's up to you to help carve new neural pathways of intimacy, comfort, safety, and trust. This is what expands your capacity to hold more—more wealth, clients, responsibility—and increases your resilience in tough emotional moments.

Signs of early attachment trauma may include the following:

1) Self-Sabotage: Inaction or perpetual procrastination.

2) Paralyzing fear: You tend to be risk avoidant and don't even try.

3) Self-doubt: Codependency, people-pleasing, self-rejection, constant fear of judgement, "good girl syndrome," imposter syndrome, and so on.

4) Lack of Clarity: Indecisiveness, confusion, and chaos in the mind.

This part could be a book in and of itself, but I will aim to give you just enough to plant the seed that if these wounds of the heart are holding you back, you can start to intellectually understand why at a deeper level, and then you can get the help you need to more deeply explore it.

17

SLAY SELF-SABOTAGE

*Many of life's failures are people who did not realize
how close they were to success when they gave up.*

—*Thomas A. Edison*

What few people know is how we all have capacity limits. This is usually defined as our comfort zone. Interestingly, your comfort zone can also be living in discomfort.

If you grew up with a family who had lots of drama, arguments, and fighting, then that is your "comfort zone" and you will likely recreate this subconsciously in your relationships.

If you grew up with worry and fear around money, scarcity, shortage, and struggle, you will likely recreate this subconsciously as an adult.

Even though you don't want these scenarios, it's what you've been programmed for, so even if you set an intention to never have those struggles, there are high chances you will recreate these unwanted experiences.

This happens because we are wired for certain experiences. Part of it is because of know-how (if we didn't learn how to have successful relationships then we won't *know how* to actually create them), and part of it is at the subconscious level (our nervous system is only calibrated to certain experiences and anything outside those causes malfunction or fight/flight mode).

FROM VICTIM TO VICTORY

Science has proven we act according to our beliefs. If deep down we believe our needs won't be met, we will actually create scenarios that reinforce this construct. This is how self-sabotage works.

As you can guess, this doesn't serve you in love, career, health, money, or any other important area of your life.

Those wounds may translate into thoughts in your business such as "People will never pay that," "What will people say when they read this post?" or "I don't want to sound like a sleazy saleswoman."

You may find you...

- Tend to do it alone
- Feel unworthy
- Are terrified of rejection and being judged
- Keep delaying or procrastinating
- Feel perpetually unclear or confused
- Are hypercritical of others

- Fear outshining others
- Find problems that make you quit
- Constantly react emotionally rather than logically
- Throw away success

The reality is that no matter how much you're aware this may be happening for you, it's hard to see it yourself when you're in the middle of it. It's even harder to make a different choice.

I see it time and time again with hundreds of students at this point, how even with the information and the strategy, without being seen and held accountable by someone else, many will ultimately self-sabotage any success they build.

Shiny Object Syndrome

A few years ago, when I felt maxed out with sales calls, program delivery, marketing, and a million other things, I started thinking life and business would be easier with a passive income course selling for $1,997 so I didn't have to do any sales calls.

I was distracted by a shiny object, and when it didn't work, I felt totally lost, shrank back, and quit (for a while).

Creating a million-dollar business will test you repeatedly. You'll want to quit. You'll want to change directions.

Sometimes it'll feel like it's not working and you'll want to pivot. You'll want to chase a new strategy that seems to solve all your problems—also known as *shiny object syndrome.*

Your entrepreneur brain will get excited about something new—a distraction.

These are the moments when you are being tested.

Most people quit when things get hard. They don't have the capacity to be there and work through the challenge in front of them, to be with the fear and the pain or the underlying dissatisfaction. What is at the root? If you can be there, you can move through it without getting distracted and move through it powerfully and quickly.

If you quit or change directions every time things get hard, you'll end up with nothing to show for years of hustle. You must stay the course, be aware of the cycles you're in, and break the ones that no longer serve you.

If every entrepreneur realized how if they would just focus on just one thing long enough and see it through, then they would have a multi-million-dollar business!

CONFUSION

Feeling "confused" and feeling petrified to make a decision, or make a wrong decision, is a trauma response. Our brain will literally short circuit when we bump up against our capacity limits.

"I don't know" is a way you may try to protect yourself from trying something new and potentially failing.

Understand though, most of this is happening sub-consciously, as a self-preservation strategy, so don't be too hard on yourself. In fact, the key to moving through unearthed trauma is self-compassion. My goal here is to bring light to patterns you may be unknowingly acting within.

For most of us, when we feel confused, we usually move on to something easier. We check social media. We watch Netflix. We numb the feeling with booze or sex or drugs. But here's what I've discovered: Feeling confused is a state of mind, and once you have awareness around this pattern, you can make feeling "confused" *a choice.*

Recognize that when you're feeling confused it's likely because you're facing something you've never faced before. Ahhhh! New territory. Inner talk might go something like: *It's okay. I'm likely feeling this way because I'm in new territory.* If you can train your brain to respond to confusion with self-compassion and a choice to get clarity of action, you will retrain your brain to expand its capacity. Any decision is better than no decision at all.

Becoming a millionaire is more about the expansion of how much you can hold—increased responsibility, fire drills, problems, questions. If your nervous system fizzles out every time you hit a problem, then you won't reach the next level.

18

PEOPLE-PLEASER WOMEN DON'T MAKE MILLIONS

There is only one way to avoid criticism: do nothing, say nothing, and be nothing.

—*Aristotle*

Also known as doormats and "good girls," agreeable women find their safety in avoiding conflict and feeling loved by everyone.

Imagine this, when you were six years old your first-grade teacher was mean to you. As soon as you walk in the door from school, you run to tell your mom about how sad you were and how you were crying on the playground after the teacher yelled at you.

Your mom stops you before you're even able to express to her what happened and tells you to go outside and play. What you didn't know is that the whole day you were at school, your infant brother was very ill. Your mom was very worried about him and at that moment she didn't have the capacity to listen to you.

Mom didn't do anything wrong here, but in that moment, you likely felt a little rejected, and depending on how often this happened throughout your childhood, you could have a large wound around feeling unmet, uncared for, unloved.

There are generally two different reactions to rejection. One is passive. A woman may find her safety in being agreeable and withdrawn.

The other reaction is aggressive. A woman may become a fighter, developing a don't-care attitude, and a shell of outer hardness.

In essence, we develop behaviors to satisfy and meet our basic needs, such as love and security.

We may even begin to mold ourselves into who we think our parents want us to be, which in turn makes us grow into adults who find our worth in what other people think of us.

This is how we become people-pleasers and codependents.

People-pleasers are conflict avoidant, so you can imagine how tough it is for them to sell.

Stating the investment and holding the space for the client to step through their fear can be quite difficult for a people-pleaser, because this woman tends to orient more towards what will be pleasing or easy for the client.

And because people-pleaser women have developed these unhealthy ways of relating to themselves and others, they also find it hard to be seen and well respected in the marketplace, also known as imposter syndrome. They constantly compare themselves to others and feel rejected as a form of self-protection.

Women tend to be stuck in comparison mode, constantly looking at what other people are doing, comparing themselves to others, what they're offering, how they look on camera, how much they're charging, how much training they have, what their certifications are, and so on.

Codependency causes us to rely on outside sources for love and worthiness.

Not being able to fill our own cups, waiting for a savior, feeling dependent on getting our needs met outside—are all codependent behaviors.

Trauma Responses

FIGHT	FLIGHT
• AGGRESSIVE • ASSERTIVE - "BULLY" • DOMINATES & CONTROLS OTHERS • DEMANDS PERFECTIONS FROM OTHERS • PURSUES POWER & CONTROL • IMPULSIVE DECISION MAKING • TEMPER & ANGRY OUTBURSTS • INCESSANT CRITICIZING & RAGING	• "WORKAHOLIC" • OVER WORRYING • OBSESSIVE AND/OR COMPULSIVE BEHAVIORS • HYPERACTIVE • ALWAYS ON THE GO & STAY BUSY • PERFECTIONIST & OVER ACHIEVER • OVER ANALYTICAL • FEELINGS OF PANIC & ANXIETY

FREEZE	FAWN
• DISSOCIATION • DEPRESSION • STRUGGLES WITH MAKING DECISIONS • BRAIN FOG • AVOIDS HUMAN CONTACT • DETACHED • FEELING SPACED OUT • HIBERNATING OR ISOLATING • LIFELESS/FEELING DEAD INSIDE	• CO-DEPENDENT • PEOPLE-PLEASING • LACK OF BOUNDARIES • HAS A HARD TIME STANDING UP FOR THEMSELVES OR SAYING "NO" • DEFERS TO OTHERS IN DECISION MAKING • DESPERATELY WANTS TO FIT IN • AVOIDS CONFLICT

GUILT USED TO RUN MY LIFE

Being the "good girl" required a high barometer to accept I was responsible for everyone and everything.

Even if I intentionally did something or not...

Even if I was part of the problem or not...

Because another person is feeling pain, I should feel guilty. I not only should feel guilty, but I should stop doing what I'm doing and focus on what THEY need.

This took me down more times than I can count.

It made me abandon my dreams.

It made me feel unworthy.

It made me hide.

Guilt is like that. It will take over. It's one of the lowest emotional vibrations you can hold.

You sabotage yourself because you don't feel worthy.

You abandon your own dreams in support of other people's dreams because it feels better to make them happy.

You listen more to what other people say you should do than your own inner voice.

You stop REACHING for more because it will make them feel uncomfortable.

You WAIT for permission to go after your dream.

When you're riddled with guilt, you can't even find your inner voice, your passions, your dreams, or your goals.

This kind of guilt made me play small, not use my voice, not make millions, choose relationships that weren't encoded with divine power, and choose jobs that weren't an expression of my soul's gifts.

It kept me following the pact of people who also feel inherently guilty for literally *everything*.

When you're riddled with guilt, you don't even know WHO you are, what you stand for, or how to OWN it.

You can't even find it because someone else told you your dream would intimidate them, make them feel small, or it would mean you don't need them anymore, or maybe you don't really care about those who've suffered.

The guilt has a hold on you. Stop that.

BOUNDARIES SAY "I'M WORTHY"

If you grew up with an unhealthy, alcoholic, codependent family system like I did, then you likely know boundaries are not encouraged in these dynamics.

We learn how to be way too open with people because we learned codependent ways of relating. We learned how to please others to get love, and saying no, which is a way of stating a boundary, doesn't usually go over well.

Then when we want to start saying no or stating boundaries as adults, we have a lot of fear people will reject us. We also may put up walls and come across harshly.

Walls reject others and sabotage relationships.

Boundaries, on the other hand, are tender, firm, loving and, for most of us, scary and vulnerable to set. Why? Because of rejection and the fear of not being loved. For many of us, we didn't learn how to set boundaries as children while still receiving love. It was either LOVE or FIGHT.

Boundaries say "I'm worthy. What I think and feel matters. I'm not wrong for how I feel. I won't allow that. Or, "More of that, please." A boundary creates a container in which a relationship can flourish.

Boundaries state personal needs.

For example...

- I need space.
- No, I don't want to do that.
- No, that doesn't feel good.
- I'd like you to respond to me.

I used to have an adverse relationship to having boundaries and needs, mostly because I was taught I was an emotional burden to my caretakers—I was too sensitive, too opinionated, too bold, too open-minded, too curious, too wise, too much of everything.

I began to resist being "needy" because their rejection hurt too much. And then I was attracted to many people who mirrored that belief back to me, so I often heard "You ask for too much."

I started stuffing my needs down and I lived most of my life trying to get my needs met out there from other people, without having an intimate and clean relationship with my own needs.

This set me up for failure in all relationships, including money and business.

Your needs will not be met if you don't know what they are, and if you don't ask for them to be met.

When you're meeting your own needs while growing your business, you're less worried about what other people think, because you're saying no to the spirit of rejection and are putting your desire to be of service before other people's opinions.

What do boundaries look and feel like?

- It's not my job to fix others.
- It's okay if others get angry.
- It's okay to say no.
- It's not my job to take responsibility for others.
- I don't have to anticipate the needs of others.
- It's my job to make myself happy and meet my needs.
- Nobody has to agree with me.
- I have a right to my own feelings.
- I am enough.

19

SLAY THE HATERS

*"You will never be criticized by someone
doing better than you."*

—Anonymous

I opened my Instagram to see a DM notification. Someone
had tagged me in their story.

Hooray! That usually means someone shared something
of mine they love to their audience.

But not this time. Today it was a hater tagging me in her
story in big letters:

> *"@7figurefemme, I'm so sick of seeing your YouTube ads say-
> ing you have a successful business. Some of your posts only
> have 34 likes, but you have 11K+ followers. Come give me
> an explanation."*

At first, my heart started to beat faster. I felt hurt. I don't even know
this woman. But she wanted to publicly shame me on her Instagram.

She didn't just DM me privately, she posted this publicly to her story!

And then I remembered how no one who is feeling content, happy, abundant, and successful in life spends time doing this. No one.

I learned this a long time ago and it has always been true for me.

Think about it. If this woman is happy in her life, with her business, with how much money she is making, with her stress levels, even in her relationships, she wouldn't feel called to start a fight with someone online.

I'm not going to lie to you. This will happen to you too. Someone out there will be so triggered by you that they will come after you.

These are the moments when you must reach down into your soul and remember why you're doing this—to be of service.

20

DECIDE TO BELIEVE

*"Imagine what would happen if you
decided to believe that you could."*

—*Jamie Kern Lima, Co-founder, IT Cosmetics*

After three years of rejections from all the major beauty companies, Jamie Kern Lima, Founder of IT Cosmetics, finally persuaded QVC to give her ten minutes of airtime to sell her product.

This was her last chance. She had to put the last of her savings into inventory for the show. All the marketing experts were telling her that she would fail unless she used flawless skin models to sell her product, but Jamie went with her gut and used models of all sizes, skin tones, and skin challenges.

Her total inventory of 6,000 units of concealer sold out in those ten minutes, and she went on to build a wildly successful company. She broke through her self-doubt because she had a deep "why" driving her—to shift the culture in the beauty industry. She made the decision to be unstoppable.

Jamie had a dream and she decided to believe she could make good on it. In 2016, Kern Lima sold IT Cosmetics to L'Oréal for $1.2 billion and has been included on the Forbes' list of "America's Richest Self-Made Women" since 2017.

When You See It But They Don't

Every single time someone asks me what I do and I say I run an online education and coaching company, they give me a look like they're trying not to roll their eyes.

"Oh really?" they say. "What does that mean exactly?"

I can tell that they think it's not a "real business."

Later in the conversation, when I tell them we regularly book over $250K a month in sales with over 75 percent profit margins, their eyes perk up. Now, they're interested.

In the beginning of my business, those were tough conversations because most people still didn't believe in online coaching or personal development as a viable business industry.

It took consistent mindset work, affirming my success, knowing God's calling on my life to serve, and building relentless confidence in my work that kept me going when things didn't seem like they were moving in the right direction.

There *will* be times like that, ya know?

Times when you wonder if it's working, whether it will work. And times when people around you will doubt you.

It's in those moments you must return to your faith and the fact you decided to believe.

OVERCOMING LIMITING BELIEFS

Limiting beliefs are simply assumptions about your reality that come from your perceptions of life experiences.

"Bad things always happen to me."

"Everyone always hurts me."

"I'm not good at technology."

"Making money is hard."

"Rich people are bad and greedy."

"I could never speak on stage."

These are common limiting beliefs that many of us have running on an endless loop through our minds and they are creating our realities. The more aware you become of these limiting beliefs you may have learned from your parents, society, your husband, or friends, the more power you have to change them.

You are not a victim of your thoughts. On the contrary, God has given you the ability to control them.

"You have the power given to you by God to control your thoughts and imagination (vision). God designed you that way on purpose" (Philippians 4:8-9).

There's a simple eight-step process to squash any limiting belief:

1. Identify the limiting behavior: procrastinating, hesitating, self-sabotaging, etc.

2. Isolate the underlying limiting belief. What do you have to believe to be true in order to keep repeating this limiting behavior?

3. Go back and find when you first developed the thought that led to your belief.

4. *Important: Where do you feel this in your body? Does that part of your body need to express itself? How would it move?*

5. Then ask yourself the benefits of holding on to this belief. How has it served you?

6. Ask yourself what the consequences have been of holding on to this belief. What have you missed out on?

7. Is there any ultimate truth to this belief? Or is it just a story? Find the reasons to prove the falsehood of the limiting belief.

8. What would God tell you about this belief? Can you see how this belief is doing nothing but limiting you from living your purpose?

9. Choose a new thought and create a new story that empowers you. Start acting as if you believe your new beliefs. Choose your new reality. Repeat daily.

"All things are possible, if only you believe."
Mark 9:23

21

INTUITION OR TRAUMA

"Each of us has an inner thermostat setting that determines how much love, success, and creativity we allow ourselves to enjoy. When we exceed our inner thermostat setting, we will often do something to sabotage ourselves, causing us to drop back into the old, familiar zone where we feel secure."

—*Gay Hendricks*

Before every expansion in my business and my life, I've literally had to "die" to myself and let go before I could move to the next stage. This required a whole beautiful mess of purging, crying, and letting go. The fear feels insurmountable. The doubts mount.

Right before every single huge investment, it feels like it's the worst possible time, and there are many serious reasons why this would be the worst decision ever!

The visible circumstances cause me to want to withdraw.

The voice inside my head says, *Pull back, Tara. Stay safe. What if it doesn't work out?*

But because I've learned over the years how before every major expansion in my life there is a major contraction, I can see it now!

It no longer has control over me. I can look it square in the eyes and say, *I see you and I'm not backing down.*

Now I know how the fear and anxiety and doubt that mounts (which is really just pointing me to the contrast between where I am in the moment and where I want to be) is an alarm bell.

It's a signal that I'm bumping up against my capacity limits— How much more am I willing to receive?

It's a sign I'm face-to-face with my trauma again, the little girl inside who is petrified because she doesn't feel the strong parent anchor and is unfamiliar territory. Unfamiliarity often feels unsafe to the little girl part of me.

Now I have an opportunity to heal within and meet that little girl's needs myself.

I've learned now how voices of reason and voices of logic will never be in alignment with my future potential.

Old trauma will sound like intuition saying, *No, this doesn't feel right. Not right now. Sometime in the future. It didn't work out before. That last investment was a waste of money.*

Have you ever said these things to yourself? I know I have.

The next step will likely never "make sense," and in fact, that's when I know that I'm on the right path!

Crossing thresholds is what I came here for. Dying to the old, feeling the grief, and resurrecting again and again.

Being confused, stuck, feeling resistant to tech and afraid to be seen online, afraid to be fully expressed, overworking, hustling—these are all ways you may choose to protect (emotional wound) and self-abandon (avoidance).

The very act of choosing to protect rather than to open and expand is an abandonment of yourself and further reaffirms your belief in your unworthiness.

Choosing to protect can look like procrastination, resistance, confusion, lack of clarity, fear of being seen, fear of tech, or fear of judgment.

You end up feeling rejected by money, wealth, and clients because you are in fact rejecting yourself first, as a form of protection.

Most of the time when you think you're pulling back because it intuitively doesn't feel good, it's really a self-sabotage tactic to keep you in your comfort zone.

I'm not saying to always say yes or lean in with every opportunity—you must be discerning—but notice if it's your intuition or if it's just trauma holding you back and trying to protect you.

Sadly, most people don't start or go all-in because they are afraid to give up something. This is called loss aversion.

It's easier to stay in a dissatisfying comfort zone than to take the risk of failing. That's really what's at stake, right? You're afraid that if you go all in, you'll fail or lose the little that you have.

If you tend to keep saying the same things over and over, year after year, and don't have different results, then your old limiting beliefs, generational patterns, and trauma may be holding you back.

YOU WON'T SELL IF YOU DON'T BUY

I had just walked my dog home from the beach in Venice Beach, Los Angeles. Ocean breezes, palm trees, the sound of the ocean, but I couldn't enjoy any of it. I was stuck in my head trying to figure out a solution. I had to get resourceful.

Earlier that day, I had gotten off a sales call with a coach who was going to teach me how to get out of the stuck hole I was in.

I knew his method was the solution. But when he told me the investment to work with him, I didn't have it.

It was a dark day for me. I had already built a successful career in corporate, was in my early 30s, had an MBA, but I didn't even have the credit available to invest $6K with this coach.

So, I did what any single adult woman does: I called my mom (lol).

I had already been trying to build my business for a couple of years and bless her heart, she was committed to believing in me even though she didn't really understand coaching or online business.

Now, my mom is not wealthy by any means, so I knew this would stretch her and that added to the pressure I felt.

But I knew I needed to do this. I needed a solution and I needed to believe this risk of investing in myself would pay off.

She loaned me the money so I could invest with this coach, and within twenty-four days I earned over $26K.

I wholeheartedly believe I wouldn't have worked as hard and had the same level of sheer determination and willpower if I had not borrowed the money from my mom.

At this point, I've invested over $500K in my personal and business development. And I know this is one of the main reasons I now experience success.

I've failed forward countless times. I've decided it will work no matter what. I've taken risks when I felt uncomfortable.

I've healed from making "bad decisions," even though nothing is bad if you learn from it. I've developed a habit of paying for solutions to problems. This is also why I can sell. I have no problem asking people to invest tens of thousands of dollars to get the solution they need. The fact is, you sell like you buy.

If you've never gasped, held your breath, said "I can't believe I'm doing this" while giving your credit card details over the phone, you're not playing big enough.

How Far You've Come

I remember a time in my life when I dreamed of visiting Paris, Marseille, and Rome; doing photo shoots by the Seine River and Eiffel Tower; and visiting the Mary Magdalene caves in Sainte Baume, Southern France.

I remember dreaming of living by the beach in Tulum, Mexico.

Or when buying a beautiful beach house in San Diego, California, was on my vision board.

I remember when Chanel, Louis Vuitton, and Gucci were brands I dreamed of being able to buy.

I remember thinking, *wouldn't it be nice if I had all the freedom to travel whenever I want? To book New York for Christmas and a New Year's Eve trip to tropical Tulum, Mexico?*

I remember when getting payment notifications on my phone from an online coaching program I created was the "holy grail" online business dream.

I remember wishing I could spend my days the way I wanted to spend them, working from my cozy home, or traveling around the world.

I can easily get caught in where I'm going and never look back at how far I've come. I can compare myself to the woman who's already earning eight figures, not realizing she's been working at it for ten years longer.

None of us have the same background, privilege, education, exposure, or culture. All of these contribute to our trajectory. We all have different things we need to overcome.

So, give yourself some credit, sis! Stop comparing your Day 1 to her Day 1,000.

Sometimes we really do need to remind ourselves that once upon a time we could only visualize, dream, hope, and wish for what we have today!

22

WE HEAL IN COMMUNITY

"There is immense power when a group of people with similar interests gets together to work toward the same goals."

—*Idowu Koyenikan*

As I write this, I'm sitting in a cabin in Big Bear Lake, California, sipping a cup of coffee. I just got tagged in a post inside our private student High Ticket Empress Facebook group where my student Rose posted that she booked $9K in one day.

She has over fifty comments on that post in just a few hours because the women inside the group are genuinely so thrilled for her.

I think about the gift Rose has with a built-in community to celebrate this win. After all, she probably doesn't have anyone else in her life building an online transformational coaching business and booking $9K in one day.

But she has *us*. Even if every other sister didn't have the same success that day, they want to cheer her on so Rose is seen in her success, and they know they will receive the same celebration when it happens for them.

THE COST OF STAYING WHERE YOU ARE

A few years ago, I hit my first $50K month. It was immediately after I joined a new group mastermind. For a year before that I stumbled in the dark. I felt jaded after a previous coaching program and scared to re-invest. I didn't know who to trust. I went off track and wasted a lot of time.

What became so clear to me was how every month before when I didn't book $50K in new sales, I lost $50K. So, you could say I lost $600K that year. If it could've been $100K a month, then I lost $1.2 million that year.

Being a part of a group gives you an injection of fuel. There are people further along than you (but not as far as your mentor) who give you the momentum to push a little harder.

It's like car racing. You can draft off the car's speed in front of you. It's using someone else's momentum and acceleration to your benefit.

When left alone, you veer off track easily. When left to your own mind, all the new bright and shiny objects look so tempting. The biggest temptation of all is to quit when things get hard. Believe me, I've done it. That's why community is so important. Community keeps us accountable and committed to our goals.

We will always be tempted in life and in business. The people who WIN, not just in finances but in fulfillment, are the ones who stay on the narrow path.

CONCLUSION

It's Time to Live the Life of Your Dreams

If there was ever a time to be more and make more money than you ever have before, that time is now. It's time to get strategic and structured.

No more playing small. It's time to go all in and trust yourself. Make the choice to become wealthy. Choose financial freedom. Start living the life where you can pay for whatever you want. It's time to step into your role as a 7-Figure Coach—the woman who has it all and has her client leads on autopilot so she can live the life of her dreams.

This time is potent and now is your moment to go all in on your online coaching business!

Go through the process of getting clear on what your offer is and clear on what your tangible end result is.

Do your beta, get testimonials, get feedback. When you start coaching paying clients, that's when it becomes real. That's when you realize, "I was made for this!"

Watch your language. Remove limiting phrases such as the following:

I can't.
I'll try.
I can't afford it.
That's too expensive.
Maybe when I'm rich I'll...
Sorry, I can't, I'm broke.

Instead, claim your voice and take up space.

Most of us are trapped with limits on what's possible.

The four-minute mile was a record that wasn't broken for DECADES. Then just forty-six days after it was finally beat, it was beat again with a time of three minutes, fifty-eight seconds. Then a year later, three runners broke the four-minute barrier in a single race.

It wasn't a physical limit. It had become a psychological limit.

God can break all limits if you spend time with Him. He wants to break generational curses and cancel the limits in your mind. He wants to give you POWER, and help you WIN.

RECOGNIZE THE NEW OPPORTUNITY OF THIS TIME

Go High End: Charge way more than you think you should and command your clients to take the biggest leap forward in their own growth. This is the greatest service you can give to them.

Become the Messaging Queen: If you want people to listen to you, then you need to master messaging. Scaling, automation, ads, and funnels (which make your life easier and juicier) don't work without succinct messaging and an incredible offer.

Leverage Funnel Automation: Online systems will help you share your genius with the world. Using an automated system, you and your team will be able to consistently close new cold leads in your high-ticket program, even during unpredictable times.

Believe Sales Is Love and Money Is Renewable: Let your passion to serve as a child of God fuel your sales frequency. If you believe sales is love, you'll love selling. Your clients will become emotionally and financially mature adults in the containers you hold for them.

Cultivate a 7-Figure Heart: Look at every setback as preparation for something bigger. Hold your inner child as you increase your visibility and cash flow.

You Are a 7-Figure Coach

The 7-Figure Coach is healthy and happy. She chooses winning over victimhood. She takes full responsibility for herself and her well-being. She helps those around her win at business and in life.

The 7-Figure Coach masters her emotions. She surrounds herself with other women who have a positive mindset. She thrives in community, serving others, and being served.

The 7-Figure Coach also takes care of her physical body. She breathes fresh air, gets sunshine, takes walks, and stays hydrated. She lets herself rest.

You are a 7-Figure Coach. Either you've already created a 7-figure coaching or consulting business from your unique expertise or you're on your way there.

You now understand how undercharging and under-earning by selling your time is not an option. You embrace the need for a business model that gives you leverage.

While there are many different ways to package information for sale—eBooks, online courses, coaching, software, and high-level mastermind groups—you understand how group coaching and automated sales processes give you the leverage you need.

Through your signature coaching program and high-level masterminds, you reach thousands all around the country and world. You position yourself as an expert in one niche to skyrocket your influence. You build your business for long-term growth.

You come from a place of service. The money often feels like a bonus. As a 7-Figure Coach, you are here to serve the world.

"Give, and you will receive. You will be given much. Pressed down, shaken together, and running over, it will spill into your lap. The way you give to others is the way God will give to you."
Luke 6:38 (NCV)

AFTERWORD

"God gives you the resources for success. But it is up to you to recognize them and use them to their fullest."

—T.D. Jakes

Have you ever thought that by turning away from the wealth that is at your door, you are actually turning away from what God is speaking into your life?

What if I told you it's totally possible to honor yourself, God's calling on your life, your feminine need for flow and nourishment, AND build a sustainable, scalable, and profitable expert coaching business?

If you're reading this book, then within you is the desire to not only walk the required mile but also to go the extra mile. At your core, you are a high producer. You exceed expectations. The only way to get to your next level is to be faithful at your current level.

If you're not living a life of deep purpose or you don't sense a calling over your life, then it doesn't matter how much money you make. Glorifying yourself never works. It's not about you—it's about God's purpose for your life.

Faithfulness is the current season you are in. Honor God at your current level, and then get expectant. One thing the Bible has taught me recently is to get EXPECTANT. Expectations produce OUTCOMES.

If you expect a desirable outcome, then you take action. If you expect poor outcomes or if you're doubtful in your thoughts and words, then you will stall, procrastinate, and avoid.

Following God's calling on your life is how you reach your goals. Remember that God can't do YOUR part. Act like it all depends on you—but know it all depends on God.

Because I grew up with family adversity (emotional abuse, alcoholism, chaos), it was very hard for me to trust anyone, never mind God. To think of surrendering my heart and life to Christ didn't fit with the new age feminine empowerment narrative I had bought into in my twenties.

I was going to do it alone. Achieve on my own. Make it happen. Manifest it. Will it into being. Allowing a Heavenly Father to help me was something I resisted. I didn't trust Him.

I hated the dogma and rules that came with religion. I was spiritual but I didn't truly walk with God.

Fast forward through a lot of success and some failure and realizing that doing life alone—without Jesus and without the fellowship of a community of people who are also walking in Christ's teachings—wasn't fulfilling.

The new age feminist community felt distorted, but I didn't know how to find my way out.

I prayed and God intervened. He's got me always, even the years I didn't turn to Him. He brought me back to the feet of Jesus. Sobbing and hungry I went, wholeheartedly hungry to know Him better and walk in His ways.

The healing on my heart is profound.

Let my words today serve as your invitation to the feet of Jesus.

Religion has become distorted. Jesus is not. Just invite him in. He will lead you. He's got you.

> *"Come to me, all of you who are tired and have heavy loads, and I will give you rest. Accept my teachings and learn from me, because I am gentle and humble in spirit, and you will find rest for your lives. The burden that I ask you to accept is easy; the load I give you to carry is light."*
> Matthew 11:28-30 (NCV)

APPENDIX: BONUS RESOURCES

These digital downloads and videos will help you level up and step into your 7-Figure Coach genius. I've included bonus resources that show the most up-to-date tactics to implement the strategies taught. As the tactics evolve, I'll update the resources. Below is a short description of each bonus resource, and they can all be found using the following web address:

www.7figurecoachbook.com/bonuses

17-Page Guidebook to High-ticket Selling

The simple 3-Step Feminine Method you need to create a profitable coaching business in record time.

Slay Self-Sabotage

Running a business with ethics, integrity, and love is a core tenet of what the *7-Figure Coach* stands for. We attract the most amazing, ambitious, brave, smart, and loving women on the planet. Our goal is to raise their voices and shatter those upper-limit self- sabotage behaviors so they can SOAR.

YOUR FREE TICKET

Anyone following my free marketing tips knows I love to overdeliver. I'm a firm believer that every piece of content I create should have exact, actionable steps to get you at least one step closer to achieving your goal.

If you liked this book, then you'll *love* the free bonus training that accompanies it. The bonus training is approximately an hour long and goes into greater detail about many of the book's concepts. I also provide many more real-world examples I did not include in the book.

The best part is because you purchased this book, you get a free ticket to watch this exclusive training!

Please Note: The training is only available for a limited time and will *not* be accessible forever.

Most of what I reveal in this training is taught exclusively to my coaching students who pay me upwards of $30K per year and agency clients who pay even more.

When you're ready for the next step, watch my free training on how I tripled my coaching sales by deleting 90 percent of my programs: https:// www.highticketempress.com

ACKNOWLEDGMENTS

To my mom, thank you for being my number-one supporter. Words can't express what your strength and faith have given me.

To my late father, thank you for always praying for me.

To my brother, thank you for always having my back.

With extreme gratitude, I want to thank all the coaches and mentors who walked before me, taught me what they know, and gave me the swift and sometimes harsh ass-kicking I needed to take myself seriously. I wouldn't be here without you.

To my entire staff, this book wouldn't have been completed without your tireless dedication to our mission and all our student successes.

To Shanda Sumpter, for being an 8-figure woman and writing the foreword for this book, but more importantly for loving Jesus and showing me how to be a Kingdom builder.

To everyone at Authors Unite who helped make the publication of this book a seamless process, my editor Sherman, Tyler, and everyone else who worked on getting this book baby into print.

To you! Thank you for buying this book and taking the time to read it and being the kind of person who invests in her development.

And lastly, to the One who transformed my life, thank you Jesus for the love, power, and grace I never knew until I knew you.

ABOUT THE AUTHOR

Tara Mullarkey went from being raised by a single mom and eventually quitting the corporate life with no job prospects to building a 7-figure enterprise online.

Back in New York City, Tara underwrote, sold, and managed over $500 million in highly leveraged loans in the corporate finance sector, worked for the largest hedge fund in the world, and also worked for a Fortune 50 company.

After retiring from Wall Street and corporate America and completing her MBA, she traveled the world, visiting India,

Thailand, Bali, Europe, Australia, New Zealand, Tulum, Nepal, and Morocco. Then she started her own online coaching business.

Tara has sold multiple millions in coaching programs and has worked with a range of 6-figure, 7-figure, and 8-figure clients in 20+ countries, including some of the top experts in their field over the last decade. She is most definitely *not* a "pop-up" business coach!

She is the Founder of High Ticket Empress, which is a blueprint for women to package up their expertise, story, education, and certifications into a premium offer and scale it online—simply and profitably. Any woman can discover how to duplicate Tara's success and turn their coaching skills into a 7-figure business—without working 24/7.

Tara has been featured in Forbes, Yahoo Finance, ABC, NBC, CBS, Fox, and The Huffington Post for her success and leadership in female entrepreneurship. She is also a proud recipient of the Two Comma Club Award.

Tara lives in San Diego, California, where she enjoys bachata dancing and Sunday morning worship services.

CPSIA information can be obtained
at www.ICGtesting.com
Printed in the USA
LVHW021741100422
715744LV00006B/23

9 781951 503574